Linguistic Philosophy

The Underlying Reality of Language and Its Philosophical Import

ESSAYS IN PHILOSOPHY

Edited by Arthur C. Danto

Norwood Russell Hanson	Observation and Explanation: A Guide to Philosophy of Science
Jerrold J. Katz	Linguistic Philosophy
Norman Malcolm	Problems of Mind
David Pears	What Is Knowledge?
Hilary Putnam	Philosophy of Logic

Linguistic Philosophy

The Underlying Reality of Language and Its Philosophical Import

by Jerrold J. Katz

London
GEORGE ALLEN & UNWIN LTD
Ruskin House   Museum Street

First published in Great Britain in 1972

ISBN 0 04 110014

The *Essays in Philosophy* series was originally published in the
United States of America as the *Harper Essays in Philosophy*.
The American edition of this book is entitled *The Underlying
Reality of Language and Its Philosophical Import*. The British
edition is a photographic copy and American spelling and usage
have been retained.

For V. V. V.

Printed in Great Britain
by Redwood Press Limited
Trowbridge, Wiltshire

Contents

Contents

Preface

I wrote this essay about five years ago for a volume
which was to be called *The Harper Guide To Philosophy*. The volume was to be a contemporary ency-
clopedia of philosophy with a chapter on each of the
main areas of contemporary philosophy written by a
specialist and designed as an introduction to the area.
After a few years, the original project was redesigned
as a series of separate essays, under the new title *Harper
Essays In Philosophy*.

The present essay is a revision of the one originally
written as the chapter on the philosophy of language
for *The Harper Guide To Philosophy*. It takes a very
partisan viewpoint on this area, that the most significant recent development for the philosophy of language is the emergence of the transformational theory
of grammar. This essay is an introduction to this theory
and to its implications for philosophy.

Specialists sometimes flatter themselves that they
could work out just the right way of presenting their

specialization so that it would be accessible to the "general reader." This essay is my attempt to do this for general readers who are at the university level and have some background in philosophy (though not necessarily very much) and none in linguistics. Those who wish to go deeper into transformational grammar and the philosophy of language based on it are provided with directive footnotes for this purpose.

I wish to thank Diane Kravif for help with the proofs.

J. J. K.

June 1971

Linguistic Philosophy

The Underlying Reality of
Language and Its
Philosophical Import

1.
On Appearance and Reality

Science and philosophy sometimes attempt to show that things are not what they seem to be on the basis of direct experience. Some of these attempts to penetrate beyond appearances to an underlying reality have only led to bogus conceptions of what is real. Others, however, have established that certain appearances are deceiving and have thereby led to genuine advances in theoretical knowledge, ranking among the supreme achievements of human intelligence that have thereby revealed a world of strangeness and beauty lying beneath the surface in the commonplace things of life.

One of the most prominent examples of an advance in knowledge brought about by an attempt to uncover an underlying reality is the atomic theory of matter. Judged by direct experience, the matter of which ordinary objects are formed appears continuous. The belief that matter is not conglomerate in nature is encouraged not only by the look and feel of ordinary objects and substances, but also by certain common sense "explanations" of their behavior. For example, water in an unbroken glass does not leak out and this is just what one would expect if the matter of both were continuous. Indeed, if it were otherwise, one might naturally expect the water to drip out. Thus, the behavior of water in this instance seems to corroborate the belief that matter is continuous. Yet, as every high school physics student knows, this belief is a vestige of an early age of speculative science and has been superseded by the Democritean conception that matter is discontinuous.

Even though the Democritean principle that matter is constituted of exceedingly small discrete particles is at variance with the way things look and feel and with aspects of our common sense understanding of how they behave, it ultimately proved to have the greatest explanatory power. Not only did it explain the same phenomena as its rival, but it could explain a good deal that its rival could not. Quite simple phenomena, like the dissolving of solids in liquid, the diffusion of gas, the non-summative volume of a mixture of alcohol and water, the interpenetration of solids, and so forth, which were a mystery on the view that matter is continuous, became quite comprehensible on the Democritean view. Taking the view that continuity is only the surface appearance of matter and that in reality it is composed of incredibly many tiny particles with empty spaces between them made it possible to explain a phenomenon like diffusion or interpenetration as a process in which the atoms of one solid, liquid, or gas migrate into another solid, liquid, or gas and occupy the spaces between its atoms. With the atomic explanation of Lavoisier's principle of conservation of matter, Dalton's formulation of modern atomic theory, and the subsequent discovery of the new elements that Dalton's theory predicted, it became obvious that the concept of atomic structure gives us a true picture of the nature of matter. Indeed, the final confirmation of the atomic theory by actual observation of large molecules with an electron microscope came as an anticlimax.

The Democritean concept of matter originated as a purely hypothetical postulation. Initially, it could only have seemed the most extravagant of fancies. It proposed to populate the universe with unbelievably many new objects. Such objects were, moreover, supposed to be invisible and yet to provide the true understanding of visible phenomena. Finally, to add insult to injury, the concept flew in the face of the plain testimony of sense experience. But when it proved to yield better predictions and explanations of the observable behavior of physical objects and substances than the concept of continuity, it received scientific acceptance. The continuity hypothesis, which once must have seemed the last word in sober science, became relegated to the status of a depiction of appearance.

Here, then, is an outstanding case where science was able to distinguish the way things appear from the way they really are. In this monograph, we will take this case as our paradigm. It will serve as a model of the appearance–reality distinction with respect to which we shall study language. The question we will seek to answer is whether language fits this model; whether language constitutes another case in which to understand the phenomena we must penetrate beyond surface appearance to a deeper, more profound reality underlying them. We shall find that this question receives an affirmative answer, that the case of the atomic theory is a sound paradigm for linguistic theory. Thus, we shall argue that natural languages have an underlying reality very different from their surface form. We shall try to show that this underlying reality can be discovered and substantiated by essentially the same method of hypothetical postulation and empirical verification that established the explanatory superiority of the atomic theory. Furthermore, we shall argue that knowledge of the underlying reality has considerable philosophical import because of the insight it gives into the solutions to some traditional philosophical problems.

2.
Two Contrasts With Wittgenstein

There were two Wittgensteins, an early Wittgenstein
and a late Wittgenstein. Comparing the two will help
to clarify my thesis that the manner in which language
appears to us (in speech and writing) is as far from
reflecting its true nature as the appearance of matter is
from reflecting its.

The early Wittgenstein, the author of *Tractatus Logico-Philosophicus*,[1] was deeply influenced by the great
German logician and philosopher Gottlob Frege and
occupied himself with one of Frege's main concerns,
the problem of logical form. The logical form of a sentence is that aspect of its structure that determines the
logical relationships into which it enters. Logical form
is whatever it is about the sentence that determines the

[1] L. Wittgenstein, *Tractatus Logico-Philosophicus* (London: Routledge &
Kegan Paul, 1922). There are many accounts of Wittgenstein's early philosophical doctrines. A particularly readable one is found in G. Pitcher, *The
Philosophy of Wittgenstein* (Englewood Cliffs, N.J.: Prentice-Hall, 1964),
part I, pp. 17–170. Pitcher also cites a number of other books on the *Tractatus Logico-Philosophicus* phase of Wittgenstein's career, cf. pp. 330–332.

possible consequences that can be deduced from it or the valid arguments in which it can appear as a conclusion.[2] A problem arises because the overt grammatical form of a sentence is often an unsafe guide to its logical form. Similiarities and differences in the overt grammatical form of sentences often do not coincide with similarities and differences in their logical form. Consider the overtly similar sentences:

(2.1)   There is a pain in my foot
(2.2)   There is a fire in my kitchen

The second sentence, together with the further premiss

(2.3)   My kitchen is in my house

implies the conclusion

(2.4)   There is a fire in my house

On the other hand, (2.1) together with the further premiss

(2.5)   My foot is in my shoe

does not imply the corresponding conclusion

(2.6)   There is a pain in my shoe

Note further that

---

[2]This characterization of logical form is Frege's. In his *Begriffsschrift, a formula language, modeled upon that of Arithmetic, for pure thought*, originally published in 1879 and reprinted in translation in J. Van Heijenoort, *From Frege to Godel* (Cambridge: Harvard University Press, 1967), pp. 1–82, Frege sets forth this conception, p. 12.

(2.7)   I have a foot which has a pain in it

and

(2.8)   I have a kitchen which has a fire in it

are, respectively, dissimilar in overt grammar to (2.1) and (2.2) and more so than are (2.1) and (2.2) to each other, yet (2.7) is the same in logical form as (2.1) and (2.8) is the same in logical form as (2.2). Wittgenstein, like Frege before him, sought some framework within which the logical form of sentences might be represented in a less misleading, more explicit, and detailed way than it is in grammatical form. The model for this framework, as for Frege's 'formula language', was mathematics.

But the later Wittgenstein, the author of the *Philosophical Investigations*[3] and one of the founders (together with Moore and Ryle) of ordinary language philosophy, abandoned this entire enterprise and erected another framework for treating the question of logical form. The early Wittgenstein had assumed that the precise representation of the logical form of a sentence is a reduction of it to a set of logical simples and their relations; the later Wittgenstein assumes that clarity about logical form or logical grammar comes not from penetrating the logical depths of sentential structure to reveal logical simples but from comparing and con-

---

[3]L. Wittgenstein, *Philosophical Investigations* (Oxford: Basil Blackwell & Mott, 1953). Again, for a readable account of the general nature of the doctrine, cf. G. Pitcher, *The Philosophy of Wittgenstein*, this time part II, pp. 171–329 and the further works mentioned on pp. 332–334.

trasting the ways in which different sentences are used in different realms of life. In the *Philosophical Investigations,* Wittgenstein wrote:

> . . . it may come to look as if there were something like a final analysis of our forms of language, and so a *single* completely resolved form of every expression. That is, as if our usual forms of expression were, essentially, unanalysed; as if there were something hidden in them that had to be brought to light. When this is done the expression is completely clarified and our problem solved. . . .
>
> [questions as to the essence of language, of propositions, of thought] . . . see in the essence, not something that already lies open to view and that becomes surveyable by a rearrangement, but something that lies *beneath* the surface. Something that lies within, which we see when we look *into* the thing, and which analysis digs out. . . .
>
> 'A proposition is a queer thing!' Here we have in germ the subliming of our whole account of logic. The tendency to assume a pure intermediary between the propositional *signs* and the facts. Or even to try to purify, to sublime, the signs themselves.—For our forms of expression prevent us in all sorts of ways from seeing that nothing out of the ordinary is involved, by sending us in pursuit of chimeras.[4]

And in *The Blue Book* he wrote:

> It seems that there are *certain definite* mental processes bound up with the working of language, processes through which alone language can function. I mean the processes of understanding and meaning.

[4]L. Wittgenstein, *Philosophical Investigations,* pp. 43^e–44^e.

The signs of our language seem dead without these mental processes; and it might seem that the only function of the signs is to induce such processes, and that these are the things we ought really to be interested in. . . .

Frege ridiculed the formalist conception of mathematics by saying that the formalists confused the unimportant thing, the sign, with the important thing, the meaning. Surely, one wishes to say, mathematics does not treat of dashes on a bit of paper. Frege's idea could be expressed thus: the propositions of mathematics, if they were just complexes of dashes, would be dead and utterly uninteresting, whereas they obviously have a kind of life. And the same, of course, could be said of any proposition: without a sense, or without a thought, a proposition would be an utterly dead and trivial thing. And further it seems clear that no adding of inorganic signs can make the proposition live. And the conclusion which one draws from this is that what must be added to the dead signs in order to make a live proposition is something immaterial, with properties different from all mere signs. But if we had to name anything which is the life of the sign, we should have to say that it was its *use*.[5]

There are, of course, a number of reasons for this change in doctrine, but the central one, as I see it, was the belief Wittgenstein expressed in the *Tractatus Logico-Philosophicus* that

Language disguises thought. So much so, that from the outward form of the clothing it is impossible to infer the form of the thought beneath it, because the outward

[5]L. Wittgenstein, *The Blue Book* (Oxford: Basil Blackwell & Mott, 1958), pp. 3–4.

form of the clothing is not designed to reveal the form of the body, but for entirely different purposes.[6]

If one believes that the logical form of a sentence, or in Wittgenstein's *Tractatus* phraseology, the thought expressed by the sentence, is irretrievably concealed behind a phonetic or orthographic disguise, then one cannot seriously continue to study the logic of sentences by trying to translate their overt grammatical form into a suitable representation of their logical form.

Moreover, if the thought is so successfully hidden by its outward form in speech or writing, such inscrutable thoughts become suspicious, taking on the air of queer or occult entities. Wittgenstein seems to have believed that to save philosophy from the Scylla of formalism, on the one hand, and from the Charybdis of Fregean occultism, on the other, it was necessary to replace the Fregean notion of logical form or meaning, which he himself had adopted in the *Tractatus*, with a new one according to which meaning lies in the public use of linguistic forms. The Fregean style of conceptual analysis sought to uncover the logical structure of thoughts expressed in sentences by exploring grammatical clues to their universal logical substructure and formulating the findings in rigorous formulas of a scientifically devised 'concept-script'.[7] Wittgenstein replaced this by a

[6]L. Wittgenstein, *Tractatus Logico-Philosophicus*, pp. 61–63.

[7]Frege wrote: ". . . for all the multiplicity of languages, mankind has a common stock of thoughts. . . . The task of logic can hardly be performed without trying to recognize the thought in its manifold guises." "On Concept and Object," in *Translations from the Philosophical Writings of Gottlob Frege*, edited by P. Geach and M. Black (Oxford: Basil Blackwell & Mott, 1952), p. 46, first footnote.

style of conceptual analysis in which we understand meaning in terms of an examination of the public features of the ways speakers actually use sentences to carry on social intercourse. This replacement of the traditional notion of logical form must have seemed the only recourse open to Wittgenstein, the only way to steer a safe course between the formalist rock and the Platonist whirlpool.

The distinction between logical form and grammatical form, between the thought or meaning of a sentence and its overt phonetic or orthographic shape, is an appearance–reality distinction. The distinction is, as I shall try to show, both a tenable one and as central to the understanding of language as the distinction between surface continuity and underlying discreteness is to the understanding of matter.

A Democritean theory of language contrasts with the early philosophy of Wittgenstein in its assumption that logical form is inaccessable. I think that to have dropped the idea of an underlying conceptual reality in language to which the study of philosophical logic addresses itself was both a tragic mistake and an unnecessary one. It was unnecessary because it was not the only assumption that might have been given up to avoid an admittedly unacceptable occultism. One could retain the idea that language has an underlying conceptual reality and instead drop the assumption that it is completely inaccessible. Thus, as opposed to Wittgenstein's early philosophy, I shall argue that logical form is accessible if one employs the proper approach to the exploration of logical substructure.

I shall argue that it *is* possible to infer the form of the thought beneath the outward form of surface grammar so long as the inference is of the same sort as that which led to our knowledge of atomic structure. To vary Wittgenstein's metaphor somewhat: While it is true that language disguises thought, the disguise fits in such a way as to enable us to frame for ourselves a facsimile of the form of the body hidden beneath if we are willing to penetrate the disguise in the way physicists penetrated the disguise in which nature presents matter to us in sense experience.

Thus, a Democritean theory of language also contrasts with the later philosophy of Wittgenstein. Within the framework of a Democritean theory, we conceive the problem of understanding the logical features of language as a problem of theory construction. Wittgenstein in his later philosophy makes it a central tenet that an understanding of the logical features of language is not to be obtained from theories. He equates such understanding with the elimination of misunderstandings that arise when we try to grasp one concept on the basis of an analogy with another, e.g., when we try to understand mental privacy in terms of physical privacy. The elimination of the misunderstanding, e.g., the solipsistic interpretation of the concept of mental privacy, is to be achieved by the philosophical activity of exhibiting the inadequacy of the analogy by revealing the misuses of language on which the analogy depends. Thus, Wittgenstein writes:

> Our investigation is therefore a grammatical one. Such an investigation sheds light on our problem by clearing

misunderstandings away. Misunderstandings concerning the use of words, caused, among other things, by certain analogies between the forms of expression in different regions of language.—Some of them can be removed by substituting one form of expression for another; this may be called an "analysis" of our forms of expression, for the process is sometimes like taking a thing apart.[8]

In the first of our quotations from the *Philosophical Investigations*, Wittgenstein berates the tendency to assume a conceptual structure intermediary between signs and facts, between words and the world, and then he goes on to berate something else, namely, the tendency to "purify, to sublime, the signs themselves." He amplifies on the latter point, saying:

On the one hand it is clear that every sentence in our language 'is in order as it is'. That is to say, we are not *striving after* an ideal, as if our ordinary vague sentences had not yet got a quite unexceptionable sense, and a perfect language awaited construction by us.— On the other hand, it seems clear that where there is sense there must be perfect order.—So there must be perfect order even in the vaguest sentence.[9]

This point cuts deeply into the rationale Frege gives for his *Begriffsschrift*, namely, that such a concept-script will be free of the imperfections and limitations of natural languages,[10] and accordingly, it also undermines

[8]L. Wittgenstein, *Philosophical Investigations*, p. 43[e].

[9]*Ibid.*, p. 45[e].

[10]In the preface to the *Begriffsschrift*, Frege wrote: "I believe that I can best make the relation of my ideography to ordinary language clear if I compare it to that which the microscope has to the eye. Because of the range of its possible uses and the versatility with which it can adapt to the most diverse circumstances, the eye is far superior to the microscope. Considered

subsequent efforts, particularly on the part of Carnap, to carry on Frege's program.[11] However, Wittgenstein did not distinguish such efforts to construct a logically perfect artificial language from efforts to construct a linguistic theory about natural languages that can represent the logical structure beneath the surface grammar of their sentences. One can agree with him that our language 'is in order as it is', that it does not contain flaws that prevent it from serving the functions for which a language is required, but, nevertheless,

as an optical instrument, to be sure, it exhibits many imperfections, which ordinarily remain unnoticed only on account of its intimate connection with our mental life. But, as soon as scientific goals demand great sharpness of resolution, the eye proves to be insufficient. The microscope, on the other hand, is perfectly suited to precisely such goals, but that is just why it is useless for all others," p. 6. The imperfections to which Frege refers are such things as "symbols . . . that seem to stand for something but have no reference, e.g. divergent infinite series," ordinary ambiguity of expressions, vagueness or imprecision of words, etc. Cf. *Translations from the Philosophical Writings of Gottlob Frege*, p. 70, and elsewhere. In my book *Semantic Theory*, (New York: Harper & Row, 1971), ch. 4, I show that failure of reference is by no means an imperfection of language but a necessary feature of linguistic expression. The same can be said of ambiguity. And vagueness or imprecision in the conditions under which words are used is not, it might be argued, even a feature of language, e.g., it is not possible to answer the question "Which is thicker, a fat noodle or two thin ones together?," but it is possible to answer "Which is greater in height, a tall man or two short men (not midgets) one standing on the shoulders of the other?." Isn't this difference in answerability a matter of the present facts about the distribution of noodle sizes vs. the distribution of human heights, not a matter of the linguistic properties of the words used? Thus, Frege's claim about imperfections in natural language is like the claim that rivers are imperfections of the earth's surface because one who doesn't know the geography can fall into them. The notion of a linguistic theory as an alternative to an ideal artificial language is thus like the suggestion that instead of rerouting rivers so people unfamiliar with the terrain do not fall into them, we simply provide a map.

[11]R. Carnap, *The Logical Syntax of Language* (London: Routledge & Kegan Paul, 1937). A non-technical exposition of this stage of Carnap's thought is found in R. Carnap, *Philosophy and Logical Syntax* (London: Kegan Paul, Trench, Trubner, 1935).

claim that to understand our language it is not enough to look at how signs are used and to cite similarities and differences in use. Because Wittgenstein confuses the attempt to rationally reconstruct languages with attempts to describe their structure, he fails to provide any reason why the latter enterprise should be renounced in favor of analyses of the uses of words that are aimed at clearing up misunderstandings.[12] His arguments against theories in the former sense, logically perfect artificial languages intended to replace natural languages (at least for logical and philosophical purposes), thus in no way undermine the case for theories in the latter sense, systems of descriptive and explanatory principles like those found in the natural sciences.

Still there is Wittgenstein's claim that overt grammatical form totally disguises the underlying logical body of a sentence. Why should we believe that we can penetrate the disguise? One reason for us to believe we can penetrate phonetic or orthographic clothing is that speakers of a natural language do exactly this when other speakers successfully communicate with them. For example, the almost identical clothing of (2.1) and (2.2) does not hide the logical differences between

[12]Wittgenstein thought of philosophical problems as a sort of intellectual illness whose cure is the fundamental aim of philosophical investigations. "The real discovery is the one that makes me capable of stopping doing philosophy when I want to.—The one that gives philosophy peace, so it is no longer tormented by questions which bring *itself* in question.—Instead, we now demonstrate a method, by examples; and the series of examples can be broken off. Problems are solved (difficulties eliminated), not a *single* problem." And he concluded, "There is not *a* philosophical method, though there are indeed methods, like different therapies." *Philosophical Investigations*, p. 51e.

them completely. Accordingly, we may suppose that in the process of learning their language speakers have acquired a system of rules for relating sound and meaning and that they use these rules to obtain their own internal representation of the thoughts of other speakers from the speech sounds through which such thoughts are expressed. We may suppose further that if in order to understand another's speech a speaker must penetrate the phonetic disguise of another's thought, and if such penetration is achieved by a system of rules that determines the thought from the phonetic shape, then a knowledge of such a system, in the form of a theory that formulates these rules, would itself uncover the underlying logical form of sentences. If linguists could discover the principles by which the speakers of a language perform the encoding and decoding of thoughts in linguistic communication, then they would succeed in doing just what Wittgenstein said was impossible.

The only objection that can now be made to our trying to find an underlying reality in language by constructing a theory about these principles is that, given that there is such an underlying reality, it cannot be uniquely determined.[13] But this is a mere *a priori* con-

[13]The philosophically sophisticated reader will note that I have omitted Quine's views which, as I understand them, are that there is no underlying reality of the sort intended here, and so, nothing for a theory of language (as opposed to grammars of particular languages or descriptions of families of languages, e.g., Indo-European Languages, Semitic Languages, and Austronesian Languages) to be a theory of. Quine's views are clearly to be distinguished from ones that grant such an underlying reality and argue its inaccessibility to theoretical representation, though on some ways of reading Quine he argues this latter position, too. Quine's view can be found in the

tention that a science of language is, in principle, impossible. It deserves no more consideration than we would give to a similar contention in other areas of science that, although the phenomena might assume lawful form on an underlying level, we cannot come to know the laws by studying the phenomena.

second chapter of his book *Word and Object* (Cambridge: M.I.T. Press, 1960), and subsequent papers. The reply on behalf of the theoretically ambitious linguist can be found in N. Chomsky, "Quine's Empirical Assumptions," *Synthese*, Vol. 19, No. 1/2, (December 1968), 53–68, and J.J. Katz, *Semantic Theory*, ch. 6.

3.
Methodological Preliminaries

An assumption about the existence of an unobservable system puts a weight on our credulity that can only be supported by proportionately strong evidence, by evidence strong enough to bear the strain. Evidence is sufficiently strong to support the assumption of an underlying reality if the evidence cannot be accounted for without such an assumption. Thus, if it can be established that the assumption is warranted by the evidence in this sense, we strain our credulity far less by accepting the unobservable system it depicts as real than we would were we to accept an alternative theory that cannot account for the facts.

To show that the assumption is warranted, we shall have to show that no theory based on the non-Democritean principle that the only significant grammatical structure of sentences is found in their surface form cannot predict and explain a sufficiently large range of grammatical properties and relations. Thus, before entertaining any hypothesis about an unobservable reality underlying the observable phenomena of surface form, we will provisionally accept the non-Democritean principle in order to see how far a theory of language based on it can take us in predicting and explaining grammatical properties and relations.

If the appearance of language is the last word on its reality, then natural languages have no structure other than what is observationally manifest in the utterances of sentences. We can give this notion 'observationally manifest' a more concrete sense if we say further that such features have a physical basis in the sound pattern of the utterance. Some observationally manifest features may be perceptually present while others may require perceptual aids like spectrographic pictures of speech. We will understand 'grammatical properties and relations' to refer to any feature of a sentence type that distinguishes its grammatical structure from that of another sentence type, e.g., the well-formedness of (2.1) and (2.2), the synonymy of (2.1) and (2.7), the entailment of (2.4) by (2.2) and (2.3), the failure of (2.1) and (2.5) to entail (2.6), and the oddity of (2.6). The claim that non-Democritean theories make is, therefore, that the prediction and explanation of such grammatical distinctions among sentence types can be carried out without referring to anything but observationally manifest features of the utterance-tokens of these types.

Democritean theories make the opposite claim, namely, that features of the physical content of the utterances that constitute the tokens of a sentence type are not, or are not in all cases, sufficient to predict and explain its grammatical properties and relations. Such theories must thus assume that a language, because it has an underlying level of structure at which we find features that enter into the explanation and prediction of grammatical distinctions but are not part of the physical content of utterances, is to be defined in terms of the rules that speakers use to encode their thoughts and to decode the utterances expressing the thoughts of others. Non-Democritean theories make the simpler assumption that a language is to be defined in terms of utterances *per se*.

Before we can compare such theories and try to show the point at which the weight of contrary evidence forces us to abandon our provisional non-Democritean assumption and posit an underlying level of grammatical structure that enables us account for the evidence, we must set up a neutral theoretical framework within which to make the comparison. Trying to make the comparison without such a common framework would be like trying to compare the continuity theory and the atomic theory without first knowing in general what counts as a physical theory about matter, i.e., without relatively clear answers to such questions as "What are the relevant phenomena to be predicted and explained?" "What kinds of causes can be used to explain such phenomena?" "What form do laws take?" "What are the methodological constraints that determine how well a theory accounts for the evidence?" and so forth.

The framework within which such questions can be clarified must start with a general notion of what type of theory concerns itself with stating the facts about the syntactic organization and the phonetic and semantic interpretations of sentences in a natural language. We call such a theory a 'grammar'. As we have pointed out, a person who has learned a language has acquired a system of rules that relates the phonetic shapes of sentences to their meaning which enables him to understand utterances and produce ones that others can understand. We also pointed out that the linguist's job is to try to propose a theory about the nature of such a system that explicates the rules that speakers use to relate sound and meaning.

The competing theories under consideration are thus theories about the nature of grammars as well as theories about the nature of language. The non-Democritean theory says that grammatical rules reflect the physical structure of utterances, while the Democritean theory says that these rules are both more abstract and more complex and involve deeper principles of linguistic organization expressing latent structure far richer than any facsimile of the physical structure of utterances. Both theories can be looked at as theories about the optimal model for the writing of particular grammars which say what form the rules of a grammar have to take, what constructs are to be used in the formulation of specific rules, and how the rules should be systematically related in a grammar. A theory of grammars in this sense is a theory of the universals of language because it restricts the kind of rules that can appear in grammars, the constructs used in their formulation, and the organization of grammars. It is also a theory of language because the rules written under one set of restrictions express different kinds of linguistic generalizations from those that are expressed by rules written under another set. Accordingly, the model that states such restrictions *ipso facto* restricts the kinds of generalizations that can be made about language and thus expresses hypotheses about the universals of language. By making certain kinds of generalizations about natural languages impossible to state in grammars and by making others necessary, such a model makes substantive claims about the inherent structure of natural languages. Because it makes such claims in the form of statements about the optimal grammar of a language, this type of theory plays a dual role and hence is referred to both as 'a theory of language' and 'a theory of grammars'.[14]

Because the competing theories of language are also theories of grammar we can judge between competing theories on the basis of an empirical investigation into the nature of grammars of natural languages. If we have strong empirical evidence that the grammar of, say, English must be written to incorporate certain generalizations and these are difficult to express in one theory of grammar, then that theory is empirically disconfirmed, and if such generalizations are easy to ex-

[14]For an interesting example of how hypotheses in the theory of grammar about the form of the rules in particular grammars express substantive claims about the structure of natural languages, see N. Chomsky, *Syntactic Structures* (The Hague: Mouton & Co., 1957), chs. 3–6; and P. Postal, "Limitations of Phrase Structure Grammars," in J.A. Fodor and J.J. Katz, eds., *The Structure of Language: Readings in the Philosophy of Language* (Englewood Cliffs, N.J.: Prentice-Hall, Inc., 1964), pp. 137–151.

press in one of the theories, then it is empirically confirmed.

To determine the empirical evidence in favor of a grammar and decide if the grammar is the best choice on the available evidence, we must compare what it predicts about the phonological, syntactic, and semantic properties and relations of the sentences in the corpus, with what fluent speakers of the language say about their phonological, syntactic, and semantic properties and relations. The set of such predictions that a grammar makes about a sentence is its *linguistic description*. The intuitive judgments of fluent speakers constitute the empirical phenomena to be predicted by linguistic descriptions. To illustrate this, consider the following examples:

(3.1)   Peter Piper picked a peck of pickled peppers
(3.2)   peppers pickled of peck a picked Piper Peter
(3.3)   tongue twisters flabbergast Peter Piper
(3.4)   what did Peter Piper pick?

Fluent speakers of English will make the following sorts of intuitive judgments about these cases:

(i)   The whole of (3.1) is a sentence of the language, but (3.2) is not.
(ii)   "Peter Piper," "a peck of pickled peppers," and "tongue twisters" are constituents of the same type, as contrasted with "picked," "a," and "of."
(iii)   Nonetheless, "Peter Piper" and "pickled peppers" differ from each other in just the way that "New York" and "metropolis" do.

(iv) "Peter Piper" in (3.1) is related to "picked" in that sentence in the same way that "tongue twisters" is related to "flabbergast" in (3.3).

(v) (3.1) is related to (3.4) but not to (3.3).

Facts such as (i)–(v) must somehow be stated in the linguistic descriptions that the rules of the grammar assign to sentences such as (3.1)–(3.4).

In high school or college English courses, a student learns grammar by learning certain informal techniques for parsing sentences. These informal techniques are rules of thumb for breaking a sentence up into its parts, classifying parts, and indicating certain relationships between them. For example, such rules say that nouns, adjectives, verbs, adverbs, and conjunctions are the basic parts of speech; that sentences of the simplest sort contain a subject and a verb, and an object (or objects) if the verb is transitive; that verbs agree with their subjects in number; that pronouns can stand for nouns and are subdivided into personal pronouns, possessive pronouns, demonstrative pronouns, interrogative pronouns, relative pronouns, etc.; that sentences are classified as declaratives, interrogatives, or imperatives depending on whether they state something, ask a question, or express a command or request; and so on. According to such "rules," the facts expressed in (i)–(v) might be accounted for in something like the following way:

(vi) (3.1) is a simple sentence because it consists of a subject, a verb, and an object in the right order, but (3.2) is not a sentence because its constituents are in the wrong order.

(vii)   "Peter Piper," "a peck of pickled peppers," and "tongue twisters" are all nouns, but "picked" is a verb, "a" an article, and "of" a preposition.

(viii) "Peter Piper" and "New York" are proper nouns, whereas "pickled peppers" and "metropolis" are common nouns.

(ix)   "Peter Piper" is the subject of "picked" in (3.1), just as "tongue twisters" is the subject of "flabbergast" in (3.3).

(x)   (3.1) is a declarative that could be an answer to the interrogative (3.4), but although (3.3) is also a declarative, it does not have the synactic form to be an answer to (3.4).

The account given in (vi)–(x) does not actually follow from parsing rules because these rules are too inexplicit and imprecise. But even if such an account can be somehow subsumed under parsing rules, using such rules to account for (i)–(v) in the manner of (vi)–(x) would be roughly like trying to account for physical phenomena using statements like "Rubbed amber attracts tiny objects," "Iron rusts if exposed to dampness," "Wood floats but stones sink," "Unsupported objects fall, the heavier the faster," etc., instead of physical laws. Worse yet, in learning such rules of thumb for parsing, one picks up certain types of grammatical information not stated in the rules themselves but absolutely essential if they are to be applied correctly. For example, such rules may list examples of nouns or noun phrases by way of illustration, but such lists do not tell us what makes something a noun or a noun phrase. Such lists cannot contain all the nouns and noun phrases, and without any criterion for distinguishing them the student is left with the job of identifying the unlisted constituents that can be subjects of sentences and with which verbs must agree. What is needed for an actual grammar is for such rough-and-ready rules to be replaced by formally precise rules that include all the information essential to their application. The degree to which the rules of a grammar are imprecisely formulated is the degree to which the rules rely on the training or fluency of those who will apply them and so omit saying things about their subject matter that could and should be said.

To avoid such reliance and the omissions it covers up, the rules of a grammar must be formal in the sense that the information they convey and their correct application depend only on the form of the symbols in the rules and on their arrangement. This requirement does not prevent the use of informal formulations of rules serving as first approximations to grammatical rules, but only ensures that they do not serve as more than this. Accordingly, the informal rules that one encounters in high school and college classes on grammar can be thought of as guides to the construction of formal grammatical rules but not as substitutes for such rules.

Besides the fact that as precision decreases we stand less of a chance of knowing what is being said about our subject, there is another reason for insisting on a formalized grammar, which has to do with certain general considerations in the methodology of science. Other things being equal, the more precise of two competing hypotheses is preferable in terms of confirmation. If imprecision has not gone beyond the point where it makes sense to raise the question of truth, the more precise hypothesis stands a better chance of being true. At first encounter, it may seem somewhat strange to hear that precision is not just a matter of clarification but also of confirmation; but this is because we have become accustomed to thinking of precision as merely a question of neatness and clarity, of how a theory is presented rather than how its truth is established. But surely precision must also figure in confirmation, since the degree of confirmation of a hypothesis depends on how well it predicts the available data and this, in turn, partly depends on the precision of its statement. If the predictions of a hypothesis are correct to three or four significant digits, it can hardly be very far wrong, whereas if the predictions are correct to only one significant digit, it stands a proportionately greater chance of error. The more precise a hypothesis is, the more severe the predictive test it can be made to pass, and the more the confirmational glory in its having passed. To put the point another way: When precise hypotheses are found to agree with the data, the chance that this agreement is merely an accidental coincidence is smaller than with less precise hypotheses.

Still another consideration shows, again, that we strive for precision in order to gain truth; *viz.*, lack of precision can mask difficulties in a false hypothesis which when uncovered might lead to a new and far more satisfactory one. Often in the history of science quite slight discrepancies between theory and fact—discrepancies that would not have been detected were the theory allowed to remain less precise than it could have been—have been the basis of conceptual revisions once a more precise version of the older theory brought to light the possibility of such difficulties. Consequently, the reason for making formalization a condition on all grammars has nothing to do with the alternatives posed by one or another competing theory of grammar but only with certain quite general requirements of scientific methodology.

But a comparison between grammars on the basis of their predictions about the data can offer us a unique best choice only if it is also made on the principle that we choose the simplest of those grammars that compare equally favorably in predictions. For the choice of any hypothesis to explain a regularity in a body of data and predict other data outside the available sample is always underdetermined by the data present when the choice has to be made. The scientist's data can never contain all the cases about which an hypothesis will make predictions, for hypotheses are not merely reports of the existing data. Rather, an hypothesis is a generalization from the existing sample of data which says that anything with the same property that qualified a case for membership in the sample will also have the common property that cases in the data were found to possess. Moreover, there will always be infinitely many alternative hypotheses compatible with the available data but which conflict with each other for the unobserved cases. For example, there are always infinitely many curves that intersect each of the data-points that represent observed values of one variable for a given value of another. Since such alternative curves differ from one another only in terms of their predictions about unknown cases and in terms of simplicity, without using considerations of simplicity to select a preferred curve there could be no justification for drawing the smoothest curve through the observed points. As this example shows, simplicity is not just a matter of elegance in formulation, but is an essential part of the process of inductive generalization.

Accordingly, simpler hypotheses must always be credited with a higher degree of confirmation on the given data, even though the more complex hypotheses conform to the data equally well. If this is not granted, one has to say that each of the infinitely many possible hypotheses from the most sublimely simple to the most ridiculously complex is equally well confirmed because each agrees equally well with the data.

Thus, as a special case of the general methodological canon that conformity to observed data plus simplicity equals inductive extrapolation, we can lay down the principle that the predictive adequacy of the set of linguistic descriptions provided by a grammar plus the simplicity of the rules that provide them constitute the adequacy of the grammar itself.

4.
The Underlying Syntactic Reality of Language

———————◆◁≫◁◆———————

As indicated above, the non-Democritean assumption about the nature of language leads to grammars whose rules only permit descriptions of linguistic features observably manifest in utterances of sentences, while the Democritean assumption leads to grammars whose rules also permit descriptions of linguistic features that are not observably manifest. The issue between these two theories of grammar—whether or not natural languages have an underlying reality—can thus also be formulated by asking which type of grammar provides the best description of languages.

The non-Democritean conception of a grammar is not just a hypothetical case, a straw man, but is, in fact, the dominant conception of a grammar in modern structural linguistics, which has been referred to as the 'taxonomic conception of grammar'.[15] Despite some

---

[15]Chomsky puts it this way, "The central methodological concern in recent American linguistics has been the precise definition of such notions as Phoneme, Morpheme, and Immediate Constituent. Almost without exception, phonemes have been thought of in relatively substantial terms as

substantive and a plethora' of terminological differences, the "Phonological Syntax" of Smith, Trager, and Hill; the Tagmemic model of Pike, Longacre, Elson, and Pickett; the Distributional Linguistics of Harris; the "Constructional Grammar" of Hockett; the "Immediate Constituent Approach" of Bloch, Wells, and others of the Yale School; the British School of Halliday and his associates; and, as well, the views of a number of "independents" such as Fries, Nida, Joos, Haugen, Bolinger, and Gleason, have—all of them—a common taxonomic conception of grammatical description.[16] Each of these views assumes that the only things to be described by a grammar are observable features exhibited in the utterances of sentences, and then goes on to erect a theory of grammatical description suitable for describing languages for which this basic assumption holds.

The taxonomic conception of grammar has two fundamental principles. First, a grammatical description of a sentence consists of an ordered inventory of the

... certain classes of sounds, while morphemes are taken to be certain classes of sequences of phonemes, and immediate constituents certain classes of morphemes. The methodological problem for linguistic theory, then, has been to provide the general criteria for making these classifications and the goal of the linguistic analysis of a particular language has been to isolate and list the particular classes, sequences, and sequences of classes, etc., which are the phonemes, morphemes, constituents of these languages. A linguistic grammar of a particular language, in this view, is an inventory of elements, and linguistics is thought of as a classificatory science." "A Transformational Approach to Syntax," in *The Structure of Language: Readings in the Philosophy of Language*, p. 212.

[16]See P. Postal, *Constituent Structure: A Study of Contemporary Models of Syntactic Description*. Publication Thirty of the Indiana University Research Center in Anthropology, Folklore, and Linguistics (Bloomington: Indiana University Press; and The Hague: Mouton & Co., 1964).

elements out of which the sentence is constructed, to-gether with a hierarchical classification of these ele-ments into phonological, syntactic, and perhaps semantic categories. Second, there exists a method for obtaining such grammatical descriptions which affords a mechanical discovery procedure in which data-cataloguing operations determine the grammatical de-scriptions for sentences of a language. The first principle says, in effect, that a grammatical description of a sentence is like a librarian's inventory of the books in a certain part of the library and that linguistics is therefore like library science. This is reasonable enough, given that all the linguistically relevant fea-tures of sentences are observable. Thus just as books may be divided into classes—these may be subsumed under broader classes, and so on—so the significant sounds that comprise a sentence may be divided into classes—these may be subsumed under broader ones, and so on. The second principle (to extend and com-plete this analogy) corresponds to the claim that it is possible to specify a mechanical procedure by which a librarian, simply by following explicit instructions, can sort and shelve books in accord with the predeter-mined system of classes. This too is reasonable enough on the assumption from which taxonomic linguists pro-ceed.

The task of constructing a discovery procedure for grammars is simply that of providing necessary and sufficient conditions for the classes into which the parts of sentences can be sorted. That is, the task consists of providing precise procedural definitions for classificational constructs like *phoneme, morpheme, word, vowel, syllable, phrase*, etc., in terms of such notions as distribution, contrast, phonetic similarity, substitutability, similarity and difference in meaning, etc., where, for example, the construct of a word may be defined by a substitution procedure which when it is applied to a part of a sentence gives a certain result just in case that part is a word. The various positions that have been taken by the taxonomic linguists mentioned above differ from each other on the questions of which of these notions are to be used to construct definitions for classificational constructs and how such definitions are to be formulated as a discovery procedure. However, linguists maintaining these positions agree that such definitions must be part of a general method which a linguist can actually apply to a corpus of utterances in arriving at grammatical descriptions of the sentences of a language, where the descriptions take the form of inventories of sentential elements suitably classified at various appropriate levels. Their assumption that all the significant features of language are exposed to perceptual view in the phonetic surface of sentences thus reflects itself in their conception of a grammatical description as a series of classifications of the parts of an utterance given by some basic segmentation of the utterance.

According to the taxonomic view, an utterance is a sequence of sounds which can be segmented into elements called *phonemes*. Corresponding sounds in different utterances of the same sentence can differ in various ways, some of which are of no linguistic relevance. For example, if you are asked to repeat what someone else has just said, your utterance will transpose the original in terms of voice quality, pitch, etc., and thus will be very different from that of a skilled mimic who can reproduce the original utterance so expertly that no one could tell the two apart. Nevertheless, anyone who speaks the language will recognize that your utterance, different as it is, is still an utterance of the same sentence. The notion of a phoneme is introduced to afford an abstraction from the linguistically irrelevant vocal features, from those that vary in different utterances of the same sentence—that is, what is not reproduced when the same sentence is repeated by different speakers with different voice quality, pitch, etc., and from phonetic differences that can be predicted from phonetic environments. A particular phoneme is thought of as a class of linguistically equivalent, significant sounds, such that exchanging one member of this class for another never converts an utterance of a sentence into an utterance of a different sentence or into a non-sentence.

Morphemes, which are the minimal syntactic units, are therefore classes of sequences of phonemes. Thus another way of characterizing a phoneme is to say it is a feature of the sound pattern of a language that differentiates morphemes in that two distinct morphemes must differ by at least one phoneme; for example, as the English morphemes "bin" and "pin" do. This leads directly to the characterization of a morpheme as a class of phoneme sequences.

The *constituents* of a sentence, its syntactic parts, are continuous segments of the sequence of morphemes that comprises it. At the lower extreme, the constituents of a sentence include each of its individual morphemes, and at the highest, the whole sequence of morphemes itself. Between these two extremes are constituents of intermediate size—the words, phrases, and clauses. They are subsequences of the whole sequence of morphemes that are neither the full sentence itself nor any individual morpheme in it. To represent the way in which the constituents of a sentence are organized hierarchically, from the whole sentence down to the individual morphemes, the syntactic description of a sentence takes the form of an inverted tree of constituents, its top embracing the whole sentence and its successively lower branches embracing successively lower-order constituents until the branching terminates with the individual morphemes.

A diagram such as

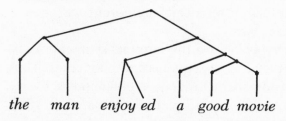

the   man   enjoy ed   a   good movie

or, equivalently, a parenthesization such as

$(((the)\ (man))\ (((enjoyed)\ (ed))\ ((a)\ ((good)\ (movie)))))$

can be used to represent the pyramidal structure of the constituents in a sentence. Each level is connected with the level below in such a fashion that there is a set of connections between any constituent on a given level and those on the next lower level that comprise its parts. Thus each successively higher level (or more inclusive parenthesization) provides a reanalysis of the constituents represented at the immediately preceding level (or next most inclusive parenthesization). The reanalysis indicates the set of constituents out of which each constituent on the immediately higher level (or in the more inclusive parenthesization) is formed. Thus a diagram or parenthesization for

(4.1)   The man enjoyed a good movie

like those above, gives an initial segmentation of (4.1) into the morphemes *the, man, enjoy, ed, a, good,* and *movie;* then a segmentation into the words and phrases *the man, enjoyed; a good movie,* and *enjoyed a good movie;* and finally the whole sentence. Each morpheme, and hence each constituent, is regarded as a sequence of phonemes.

However, such diagrams are not complete representations of the syntax of sentences because they fail to specify the character of the classes to which the constituents are assigned. To accomplish this, it is necessary to label the nodes of such tree diagrams, thereby indicating the nature of the syntactic class to which the sequence of morphemes dominated by each node belongs. Thus for (4.1) we would have

(4.2)

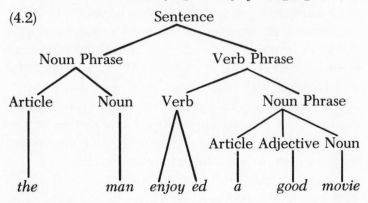

This diagram, which is referred to as a *phrase marker*, provides us with categorical information: for example, that both "the" and "a" are articles and hence constituents of the same type; that both "man" and "movie" are nouns and hence constituents of the same type; that "enjoyed" is a verb, and "good" an adjective and hence they are constituents of different types; and so on. Thus, phrase markers not only segment a string of morphemes into constituents, but also specify what the syntactic type is of each of the constituents, which constituents belong to the same type and which to different types, and which types are included as subtypes of which others.

Thus taxonomic theorists conceive of linguistic description at the phonological and syntactic levels as segmentation and classification beginning from a catalogue of speech sounds and proceeding through various stages of reclassification of syntactic constituents. The non-Democritean assumption that underlies this conception of phonological and syntactic structure also un-

derlies the taxonomic theorist's account of meaning.
Since, linguists who adopt the view that the linguistic
structure of a sentence is manifest in its observable
form cannot represent the meaning of a sentence in
terms of further taxonomic analysis, there being no further classificational structure, they must formulate
their conception of meaning in essentially behavioristic
terms. Just as they hold that all features of phonological
and syntactic structure are open to plain view, so they
also hold that no aspect of semantic structure is hidden
and that meaning must also be explained in terms of
publicly observable aspects of the use of utterances,
without an appeal to anything mentalistic or private.
Thus the meaning of sentences must be dealt with in
terms of what they refer to in the environment, what
stimuli prompt their occurrence, and what responses
they elicit. We shall return to this treatment of meaning
in the next section, after we have considered the
adequacy of the taxonomic treatment of syntax.

If the rules of the syntactic component of a grammar
are to be formal rules and are also to produce linguistic
descriptions of the sort prescribed by the taxonomic
theory of grammar, then each of these rules must be an
instruction that a certain symbol can be rewritten or
replaced by another symbol in a certain specified context. The general form of such rules is

(4.3) $XAY \rightarrow XBY$, where B is neither null nor identical to A.

Rules of this form say that the category A has the member B in the context X——Y. The syntactic component

consists of a set of such rules, each of which specifies the membership of some constituent or phrase category in some context.

Such rules yield derivations of sentences just as the rules of a mathematical system yield derivations of theorems, except, of course, that in a grammar no truth claim is involved. These grammatical derivations can in turn be converted into phrase markers by a uniform procedure of a completely mechanical nature. Thus the full set of these rules provides linguistic descriptions of the taxonomic variety.

Suppose, for the purposes of illustration, that we take the syntactic component of a grammar for the language L to consist of just the following rules:

(4.4)   (i) $S \rightarrow AB$
         (ii) $A \rightarrow cd$
         (iii) $B \rightarrow ef$

The lower case letters in (4.4) can be thought of as the symbols that represent the morphemes of L, and the set of all such symbols in the syntactic component can be called the *terminal vocabulary* of L. The upper case letters can be thought of as the symbols that represent the syntactic categories to which strings of terminal symbols belong and can be called *nonterminal symbols*. The symbol "S" can be introduced into the syntactic component as an *initial symbol* for starting derivations or (in analogy to a mathematical system) as an axiom to which rules can apply. From (4.4) we can generate a derivation of a sentence in L by writing down the initial symbol "S" as its first line and then applying (4.4)(i) to this line to form the next line and so on, until we reach a string of symbols that consists exclusively of terminal symbols and thus cannot be further rewritten. The sequence of strings of symbols from the terminal and nonterminal vocabularies that can be constructed in this manner is called a *derivation* of the string of terminal symbols that appear as the last line. Accordingly, when the rules in (4.4) are applied in the order (i), (ii), (iii), they yield the derivation

(4.5) S
          $A\,B$
          $c\,d\,B$
          $c\,d\,e\,f$

of the string "*cdef*." To convert this and other derivations into phrase markers that make explicit the way in which the rules classify strings of morphemes into syntactic categories, we have the following procedure:

(4.6)   (i) Begin with the first line of a derivation and work down to the last, connecting each symbol on a line i with its corresponding identity on line $i + 1$ or with the symbol (or symbols) on line $i + 1$ that has replaced it, as determined by the rule by which line i + 1 is obtained from line i.

(ii) Reduce all branches of the form x-z-z- . . . -z-y to branches of the form x-z-y.

By applying (4.6)(i) to (4.5), we obtain

(4.7)

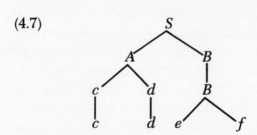

and by applying (4.6)(ii) to (4.7) we obtain this phrase marker:

(4.8)

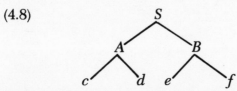

Notice, however, that the rules in (4.4) can also be applied in the order (i), (iii), (ii) to yield the alternative derivation

(4.9)   S
         A B
         A e f
         c d e f

which by (4.6)(i) becomes

(4.10)

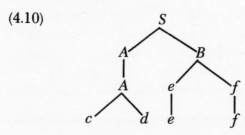

(4.10), by (4.6)(ii), is also converted into (4.8).

Derivations (4.5) and (4.9), and (correspondingly) (4.7) and (4.10) differ only in the order in which the symbols have been rewritten—i.e., the order in which the rules in (4.4) were applied. They do not differ in any linguistically significant way, since both reduce to (4.8) and thus provide the same segmentation and classification of the string *"cdef."* Thus the phrase marker (4.8) represents the class of equivalent derivations of *"cdef"* with respect to the rules (4.4). Suppose that we interpret *"S"* as the syntactic category *Sentence,* *"A"* as the category *Noun Phrase,* *"B"* as the category *Verb Phrase,* *"c"* as the morpheme *the,* *"d"* as *child,* *"e"* as *enjoys,* and *"f"* as *cookies.* We can then regard (4.5) and (4.9) as alternative, equivalent derivations of

(4.11)   The child enjoys cookies

whose taxonomic structure is described by the unique phrase marker (4.8). With this interpretation of the symbols in (4.8), this phrase marker specifies that (4.11) is a sentence, that its first two constituents form a noun phrase, and that its last two form a verb phrase. In general, the category to which a particular substring of morphemes belongs can be read off from a phrase marker according to the following definition:

(4.12)   The string of morphemes z belongs to the category C if and only if z is traceable back to a node labeled C in the phrase marker where z

occurs as a continuous substring of the string of its terminal symbol and where C dominates only z.

The condition that only (but not all) continuous substrings of a sentence are constituents of that sentence is obviously necessary within this framework, since without it we would either have no general way to read off the constituents and their category membership from phrase markers, or we would read off incorrect membership relations.

Some ambiguities in sentences and constituents are predicted when syntactic rules of the form (4.3), together with the procedure (4.6), assign two or more nonequivalent phrase markers to a given sentence. Thus the sentence

(4.13)   Children enjoy good candy and cake

receives both the phrase marker

(4.14)

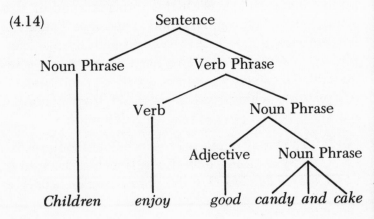

and the phrase marker

(4.15)

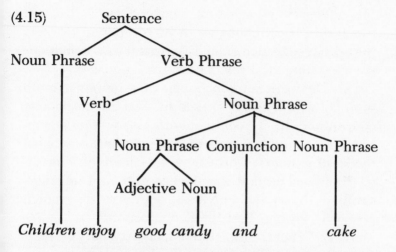

and is, accordingly, predicted as ambiguous.

Grammatical relations, such as *subject–verb* and *verb–object*, can be determined on the basis of phrase markers, if suitable definitions for such relations are given in terms of configurations of symbols in phrase markers. For example, we may say that a substring of terminal symbols z_1 *is the subject of the substring* z_2 with respect to the phrase marker W just in case z_1 is traceable back to a node α labeled *Noun Phrase*, z_2 is traceable back to a node β labeled *Verb*, β is dominated by a node labeled *Verb Phrase*, and α β is dominated by a node labeled *Sentence*. Such a definition would capture the unique syntactic character of this relation and would permit us to make such generalizations as, for example, that "the man" in (4.2) is the

subject of "enjoyed" and that "children" in (4.14) and
(4.15) is the subject of "enjoys." It will be a condition on
the adequacy of a set of syntactic rules that the
categorical descriptions given by the phrase markers
they produce be rich enough to permit such definitions
for all grammatical relations in the language.

The Democritean conception of a grammar is no
more a hypothetical case than its rival, the taxonomic
conception. In its contemporary form, the Democritean conception is embodied in the transformational
model of grammar[17] originated by Chomsky, while in
its traditional form, it is embodied in the seventeenth-
century theory of universal grammar developed,
primarily, by the Port-Royal philosophers and grammarians.[18] Thus the roots of the modern theory of transformational grammar are firmly planted in the
tradition of continental rationalist thought, whereas the
roots of the taxonomic theory are firmly set in nine-
teenth-century historical linguistics and early twentieth-century empiricist and behaviorist reactions to
the universal grammar.[19]

The fundamental insight on which the Port-Royal
Grammaire générale et raisonnée is based is that the
meaning or logical form of a sentence bears no direct
or systematic relation to the syntactic structure exhibited in the form of utterances of the sentence but that

[17]See "A Transformational Approach to Syntax" (see footnote 15) and
Syntactic Structures (see footnote 14) for comprehensive statements of
Chomsky's original formulation of the transformational model of grammar.
[18]See the Port-Royal *Grammaire générale et raisonnée*, 1660.
[19]For discussion, see N. Chomsky, *Cartesian Linguistics* (New York:
Harper & Row, 1966).

it is directly and systematically related to an underlying syntactic structure of which the observable structure of the sentence is itself a function. We use the terms 'deep structure' and 'surface structure' to refer, respectively, to this hypothesized, underlying syntactic reality and to the observable syntactic organization that sentences manifest in the form of utterances.[20] With this terminology, we can put the basic insight of these philosophers and linguists as follows: A description of the surface structure of sentences does not suffice to account for all its syntactic and semantic features; a description of their deep structure is required for this, and is also required to account for the character of the surface structure itself. The terms 'deep structure' and 'surface structure' may be thought of as the counterparts in linguistics of terms that are used in other sciences to mark an appearance-reality distinction, for example, "genotype" and "phenotype" in genetics.

This insight can be brought out, in rough form, with one of the examples discussed by the authors of the Port-Royal grammar:

(4.16)   Invisible God created the visible world.

They observe that (4.16) has a surface structure of a subject-predicate sentence like

[20]The terms 'deep structure' and 'surface structure' thus refer to aspects of linguistic phenomena. Shortly, we shall introduce the terms 'underlying phrase marker' and 'superficial phrase marker' as labels for the formal objects in a grammar that serve, respectively, as a representation of the syntax of deep structure and as a representation of the syntax of surface structure.

(4.17)   God is good

but that (4.16), unlike (4.17), has a subject and predicate that are both complex. They point out, further, that the meaning of (4.16) and of other complex sentences is expressed in an n-tuple of underlying judgments, one of which is principal and the others accessory. In the case of (4.16), the principal underlying judgment is

(4.18)   God created the world

and there are two accessory ones,

(4.19)   God is invisible
(4.20)   The world is visible

They go on to say that (4.19) and (4.20)

> ... are frequently in the mind, without being expressed, as in the above-mentioned example. But sometimes they are distinctly marked, and therein consists the use of the relative: As when I reduce the said example to these terms:

(4.21)   God who is invisible created the world which is visible

> The property therefore of the relative consists in this, that the proposition, into which it enters, shall consti-tute a part of the subject, or of the attribute predicate of another position.[21]

This amounts to the proposal that (4.16) has a deep structure:

---

[21] *Grammaire générale et raisonnée*, ch. ix.

(4.22)

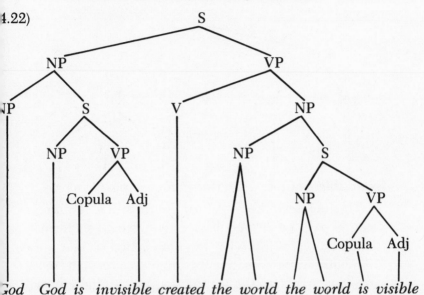

What is dominated by the two occurrences of "*S*" that are themselves dominated by something else represents the accessory judgments, and the rest of (4.22) represents the principal judgment.[22] Moreover, (4.22) also underlies (4.21), since the relative pronouns "who" and "which" stand, respectively, for the first and second repeated Noun Phrases (i.e., the second occurrence of "God" and the second occurrence of "the world") in (4.22). Somehow by operations of rearrangement and deletion, although the Port-Royal grammar does not say exactly how, the deep structure represented by (4.22) is connected to the surface structure that is represented by (4.23)

[22] *Ibid.*

(4.23)

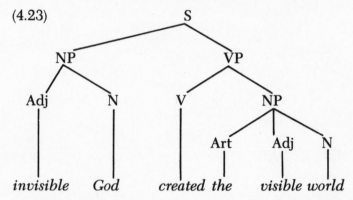

The modern theory of transformational grammar can, in part, be viewed as an attempt to give a formalized account of just what this connection is. The work of modern transformational grammarians exploits modern logic to obtain the technical apparatus for a formal account of this relation. The writers of the Port-Royal grammar could not obtain appropriate formal apparatus from what was known about logic in their day. We shall now consider the modern theory of transformational grammar, concentrating on how it formulates the concepts of deep and surface structure and on what it says about how such structures are related.

In taxonomic theory, the grammar of a natural language is conceived of as an elaborate data-cataloguing system, similar to book classification schemes in library science. In transformational theory, a grammar is conceived of as a theory that explains how speakers can associate acoustic signals with the meaning those signals have in the language, a theory similar in form to theories in other sciences that explain a body of data by showing that it can be deduced from general principles about the structure of objects which provide the reason why the facts are as they are. Thus while the model on which the taxonomic grammarian bases his conception of a grammar is a scheme like the Dewey Decimal System, the model on which the transformational grammarian bases his is a theory like the atomic theory. Accordingly, on the transformationalist conception, a grammar is a theory about the system of linguistic rules that speakers have internalized in the process of acquiring a language.[23] The significance of this difference between the tranformationalist and taxonomic theories is that only in the tranformationalist theory is there a place for deep structure, namely as a structure recursively represented in such a system of internalized linguistic rules.

Just as the physicist distinguishes between the nature of matter and its observable behavior, so the transformationalist distinguishes between the speaker's *linguistic competence* (the internalized rules that he knows) and his *linguistic performance* (what he does on

[23]The reason the transformationalist takes a grammar to be a theory about the speaker's internalized system of linguistic rules is this. First, the subject matter of a grammar cannot be identified with any historically real set of utterances, since any such set is only an exceedingly small finite sample of the infinite set of sentences of the language. Accordingly, the language has no objective existence apart from the internalized knowledge process. Second, this knowledge extends far beyond the corpus of sentences which the speaker has previously encountered, i.e., it is the ability to produce and understand new sentences, and moreover, ones that bear no direct physical similarity or analogy to those in his past experience. Thus the predictive ability to identify and understand sentences outside the set of those he has heard before makes it necessary to assume that the internalized knowledge which affords this predictive ability takes the form of a system of (linguistic) rules.

the basis of knowing such rules).[24] A grammar, then, is a theoretical statement of what speakers know about the inherent structure of their language, and thus of their linguistic competence rather than their linguistic performance, though linguistic performance provides all the empirical data for the investigation of competence.

The most remarkable fact about human speech communication is that, except for clichés and bits of social ritual like "How do you do?," the sentences we speak and hear daily are new sentences that bear little or no physical resemblance to familiar ones. Yet we understand almost every new sentence we encounter and our understanding is immediate. This is in striking contrast to our attempts at understanding new machines or gadgets, which often take considerable time and effort, and sometimes never succeed at all. Linguistic competence is the source of the creativity that makes such understanding possible, and the way this creativity operates suggests two principles to the transformationalist. First, the speaker's internalized rules must recursively generate[25] each of the infinitely many sen-

[24]Further discussion of the notions of linguistic competence and linguistic performance can be found in N. Chomsky, *Aspects of the Theory of Syntax* (Cambridge: M.I.T. Press, 1965), ch. I, secs. 1 and 2; and in G.A. Miller and N. Chomsky, "Finitary Models of Language Users," in *Handbook of Mathematical Psychology*, R.D. Luce, R. Bush, and E. Galanter, eds., vol. II (New York: John Wiley, 1963).

[25]The term 'generate' is a technical term, familiar from logic: cf. E.L. Post, "Recursively Enumerable Sets of Positive Integers and Their Decision Problems," *Bulletin of the American Mathematical Society*, vol. 50, No. 5 (May 1955), 284–316; N. Chomsky, "On Certain Formal Properties of Grammars," *Information and Control*, vol. 2, No. 2 (June 1959), 137–167.

tences of his language, so that a new sentence, though new in the sense that no utterance of it has yet occurred, is not new in the sense of being outside the set of sentences defined by these rules. Second, these rules must embody a general function for associating the phonetic representation of acoustic signals with their meaning. Thus, it is this function, operating in the generation of sentences, that makes immediate understanding of new sentences possible.

A transformational grammar is therefore an explication of linguistic competence within the framework of these principles. As such, it consists of three components: a *syntactic component,* a *phonological component,* and a *semantic component.* The syntactic component is a system of rules that generates abstract formal objects that comprise the input to the other components and which are interpreted by them. It consists of two subcomponents, one of which is an unordered set of rewriting rules (as described in (4.3)) and the other an ordered set of *transformational rules;* the former is called the *constituent structure subcomponent,* or the *base,* and the latter the *transformational subcomponent.* The rules in the constituent structure subcomponent generate an infinite set of phrase markers, which are referred to as *underlying phrase markers* because they represent the deep structure of sentences. Thus one crucial difference between the taxonomic and transformational conceptions of a grammar is that, in the former, rewriting rules generate the representations of surface structure while in the latter these rules generate the representations of deep structure. (We shall return to explore the consequences of this difference later.) The underlying phrase markers are operated on by transformational rules, which map phrase markers into new phrase markers, and convert them into *derived phrase markers.* The final derived phrase marker in any sequence of transformational operations is called the· *superficial phrase marker* and is intended to represent the surface structure of the sentence. The set consisting of all and only those underlying phrase markers that are transformationally mapped into a given superficial phrase marker, together with that superficial phrase marker, comprises the *syntactic description* of the sentence. The number of such underlying phrase markers determines the degree of syntactic ambiguity attributed by the grammar to the sentence.

The underlying phrase markers in a syntactic description form the input to the semantic component, which assigns to each a *semantic interpretation;* the superficial phrase marker in a syntactic description forms the input to the phonological component, which assigns it a *phonetic interpretation.* Therefore, the associations which speakers make in communicating between acoustic signals and meanings are reconstructed by the pairings of phonetic and semantic interpretations which are established by a transformational grammar. The two interpretations are paired by virtue of the fact that the phrase marker receiving the phonetic interpretation is transformationally related to the one receiving the semantic interpretation.

In terms of the above-mentioned characterizations of the taxonomic and transformational conceptions of a grammar, the basic distinction between them is this: The syntactic component of a taxonomic grammar generates for each sentence a single phrase marker which must contain all syntactic information required for both its phonological and semantic description. On the other hand, the syntactic component of a transformational grammar generates two or more phrase markers for each sentence, one of which must contain all the information required for its phonological description, and others of which must contain all the information required for its semantic description. Here I am using the term 'sentence' to indicate only syntactically unambiguous sentences, since both types of grammar can generate more than one phrase marker for a syntactically ambiguous sentence.[26]

Before comparing these two types of grammar on the basis of this distinction, let us make this discussion of the transformational relation between underlying and superficial phrase markers more concrete by seeing how a transformational grammar would specify the relation between (4.22) and (4.23), originally discovered by the

---

[26]This statement has to be qualified. Actually, as will be seen later in this chapter in connection with the discussion of example (4.62), a taxonomic grammar cannot generate more than one phrase marker for cases where the syntactic ambiguity is not concretely manifested in the surface structure of the sentence. Only in cases where the syntactic ambiguity is exhibited in the segmentation and classification of the surface form of a sentence can taxonomic grammars generate a phrase marker corresponding to each term of the ambiguity.

authors of the Port-Royal grammar.

The underlying phrase marker (4.22) can be generated by the following fragment of the constituent structure subcomponent:[27]

(4.24)   **(R1)**   S → NP Pred-Phrase

   (R2)   Pred-Phrase → Aux VP (Place)(Time)

   (R3) $\text{VP} \rightarrow \begin{cases} \text{Copula Pred} \\ \text{V} \begin{cases} \text{(NP) (Prep-Phrase) (Prep-Phrase) (Manner)} \\ \text{Pred} \\ \text{S} \end{cases} \end{cases}$

   (R4)   NP → (Art) N (S)

   (R5) $\text{Pred} \rightarrow \begin{cases} \text{Adjective} \\ \text{(like) Pred-Nominal} \end{cases}$

   (R6)   Aux → Tense (M)(Aspect)

   (R7)   V → CS

   (R8)   N → CS

   (R9)   Adjective → CS

   (R10)   Art → CS

   LEXICON   [*the* [+Art, +Def, ...]]
             [*God* [+N, +Count, ...]]
             [*create* [+V, +__NP, ...]]
             [*visible* [+Adjective, ...]]
             [*invisible* [+Adjective, ...]]

where a string of symbols in a derivation that contains only symbols occurring in the rules (R1)–(R10) and that cannot be further rewritten by these rules is called a

---

[27]These rules are adapted from those in ch. 2, sec. 3, Chomsky, *Aspects of the Theory of Syntax* (see footnote 24). They are intended for purposes of illustration, and are not set down as final formulations.

preterminal string. A terminal string can be obtained from a preterminal string by inserting a lexical entry in accord with the lexical substitution rule:[28]

(4.25)   If CS is a complex symbol of a preterminal string and $[D \, [C]]$ is a lexicon entry, then CS can be replaced by D just in case C is not distinct from CS.

The transformational subcomponent contains transformational rules something like these:[29]

(4.26) (R1) $X - NP_1 - NP_2 - \text{Copula} - A - Y \Rightarrow$
$X - NP_1 - \text{wh}[NP_2] - \text{Copula} - A - Y,$
where $NP_1 = NP_2$.

(R2) $X - \text{wh}[D \, [+N, +\text{Animate}, \ldots]] - Y \Rightarrow$
$X - \text{who} - Y$

(R3) $X - \text{wh}[D \, [+N, -\text{Animate}, \ldots]] - Y \Rightarrow$
$X - \text{which} - Y$

(R4) $X - NP - \left\{ \begin{array}{c} who \\ which \end{array} \right\} - \text{Copula} - A - Y \Rightarrow$
$X - (\text{Art}) \, A \, N - Y,$
where NP dominates (Art) and N.

(4.26) applies to (4.22) because the string of terminal symbols in (4.22) is analyzed as an instance of the schema to the left of the double arrow in (4.26)(R1). But note that since (4.22) analyzes this string in two ways as an instance of this schema, i.e., either as

	God	*God*	*is*	*invisible*	*ed create the world the world is visible*
X	NP₁	NP₂	Cp	A	Y

[28]See Chomsky's discussion in ch. 2, sec. 2.3.3., in *Aspects of the Theory of Syntax*.
[29]See ch. 4, sec. 2.2, Chomsky, *Aspects of the Theory of Syntax*.

or as

God God is invisible ed create	the world	the world	is	visible	
X	NP₁	NP₂	Cp	A	Y

(4.26)(R1) can be applied twice to (4.22) to yield a derived phrase marker, which by (4.26)(R2) and (4.26)(R3) becomes[30]

(4.27)

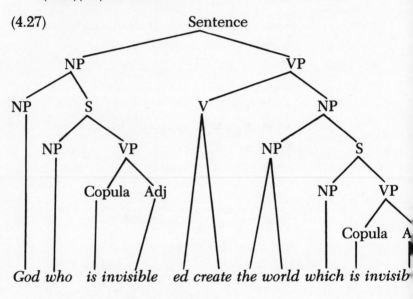

which, it will be noted, is the superficial phrase marker for (4.21). Now, (4.26)(R4) deletes the relative pronouns

---

[30]A derived phrase marker is any phrase marker that results from the operation of transformations. The superficial phrase marker is, then, the final derived phrase marker.

and permutes the adjective in front of the noun, i.e., between the noun and the article if there is one. This gives the superficial phrase marker for (4.16), *viz.*, (4.23).

Thus, (4.16) and (4.21) have the same underlying phrase marker, which means that the grammar predicts that they are paraphrases, for since they have the same underlying phrase marker, they must receive the same semantic interpretation. Moreover, the relative pronouns in (4.21), as shown by (4.27), represent the subject nouns of the two 'accessory judgments', (4.19) and (4.20), in the form of phrase marker parts in (4.22). This explicates the claim about the use of relatives made by the authors of the Port-Royal grammar. Accordingly, just as the assignment of the same underlying phrase marker to both (4.16) and (4.21) shows that their deep structure is the same, so the assignment of different superficial phrase markers, (4.23) and (4.27), respectively, shows that their surface structures differ (and also, to a certain extent, shows how they differ). The application of the phonological component to (4.23) and (4.27) will produce phonetic interpretations that show how else their surface structures differ.

The foregoing discussion is not offered as an argument against the taxonomic theory of grammar, but rather as an illustration of how the Port-Royal theory of deep and surface structure can be formalized within modern transformational grammar. Clearly, however, the explanation of relative pronouns and of the origin of adjectival constructions as derived from relative clauses, as well as the explanation of the paraphrase relation between sentences such as (4.16) and (4.21), can be cited as evidence in favor of the Port-Royal and transformationalist hypothesis about deep structure. The taxonomic theory cannot give as revealing and natural an explanation of such facts, since such an explanation depends on a sentence receiving more than one phrase marker (where these play no role in marking an ambiguity) and on these phrase markers having certain formal relations to one another, as specified in their transformational history.[31]

Now let us consider some further evidence for transformational grammars based on the same limitation of taxonomic grammars. Consider first some cases where a pair of expressions or sentences have virtually identical surface structures but where nonetheless the expressions or sentences differ syntactically from each other in ways that can only be revealed by an underlying phrase marker which exhibits their deep structure.

Jespersen distinguished between the expressions in (4.28)(i) and (ii):

(4.28)   (i) the doctor's arrival, the arrival of the doctor, . . .

   (ii) the doctor's house, the house of the doctor, . . .

He pointed out that in the sentence structures underlying (4.28)(i) "doctor" is the subject of the verb "arrive,"

---

[31]The notion of transformational history is reconstructed by the concept of a *Transformation-marker,* or *T-marker.* For a discussion, see J.J. Katz and P. Postal, *An Integrated Theory of Linguistic Descriptions* (Cambridge: M.I.T. Press, 1964), ch. 3; and ch. 3 of *Aspects of the Theory of Syntax.*

but that in the sentence structures underlying (4.28)(ii) there are no corresponding verb forms of the noun "house" of which "doctor" is the subject.[32] Taxonomic linguists have criticized Jespersen's distinction as a distortion and an unnecessary complication. But Jespersen is correct, and it is just the taxonomic linguist's preconception about the nature of grammatical analysis—according to which (4.28)(i) must be treated on the model of (4.28)(ii) and classified as an article, followed by a noun standing in a possessive relationship to another noun—that leads to a distortion and unwarranted simplification of the facts. In a transformational grammar, the expressions in (4.28)(i) are derived from a sentence whose underlying phrase marker is:

(4.29)

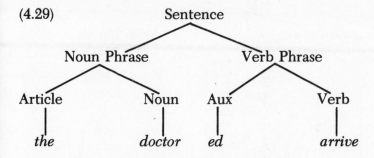

This phrase marker is operated on by what are called *nominalizing transformations* to provide the two noun phrases in (4.28)(i).[33] This explains why the two expres-

---

[32]See O. Jespersen, *Essentials of English Grammar* (New York: Holt, 1933), ch. xxx, on what Jespersen calls nexus-substantives.

[33]So-called because they make noun phrases out of sentence structures. See R.B. Lees, *The Grammar of English Nominalizations.* Publication Twelve of the Indiana University Research Center in Anthropology, Folk-

sions in (4.28)(i) are paraphrases, and why we can have adverbial modification in (4.28)(i) but not in (4.28)(ii). Thus we find

(4.30)   the doctor's sudden arrival, the doctor's quick arrival, . . . the doctor's large house, the doctor's heavy house, . . .

but no such forms as

(4.31)   the doctor's sudden house, the doctor's quick house, . . . the doctor's large arrival, the doctor's heavy arrival, . . .

The underlying phrase marker for (4.28)(ii) is

(4.32)

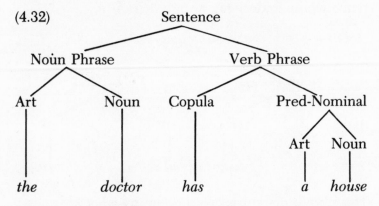

Different nominalizing transformations give the first and second cases in (4.28)(ii) when applied to (4.32), which explains why these cases, too, are paraphrases.

lore, and Linguistics (Bloomington: Indiana University Press, 1960); and *An Integrated Theory of Linguistic Descriptions,* ch. 4 (cited in full in footnote 31).

Finally, we may observe that the transformational treatment of (4.28)(i) and (4.28)(ii) explains why corresponding cases of the two sorts cannot be conjoined to form grammatically well-formed constructions. For example, we do not find grammatical constructions like

(4.33)   the doctor's arrival and house, the arrival and house of the doctor, . . .

but we do find ones like

(4.34)   the doctor's arrival and departure, the arrival and stay of the doctor, . . .

since conjunction with "and" requires that the syntactic structure of the constituents conjoined be identical, as the corresponding cases in (4.28)(i) and (4.28)(ii) are not. But the taxonomic linguist will analyze (4.28)(i) and (4.28)(ii) as identical in syntactic structure and therefore as capable of being conjoined with "and." This, of course, means that he will falsely predict that the sentences in (4.33) are perfectly grammatical.

Another case of the same type is provided by the sentences

(4.35)   John is easy to leave
(4.36)   John is eager to leave

On the taxonomic theory, (4.35) and (4.36) receive essentially the same description, since a taxonomic description is a single labeled bracketing that segments a sentence into continuous substrings, marked as constituents, and classifies them into one or another syntactic category. This description would be a phrase marker of the form

(4.37)

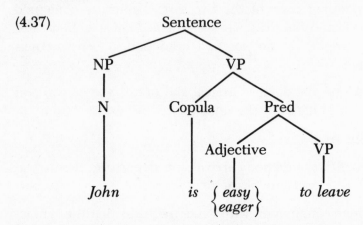

However, it is apparent to any fluent speaker of English that there is an important syntactic difference between (4.35) and (4.36) which (4.37) does not reflect. In (4.35) "John" is the object of the verb "leave." That is, "John" bears the same relation to "leave" in (4.35) as it does to "left" in (4.38):

(4.38)   Mary left John

But in (4.36) "John" is the subject of the verb "leave." That is, "John" bears the same relation to "leave" in (4.36) that "Mary" bears to "left" in (4.38). This fact can be simply explained on transformational theory. On this theory, although (4.37) will be the superficial phrase marker for both (4.35) and (4.36), these sentences will have different underlying phrase markers, *viz.*,

(4.39)

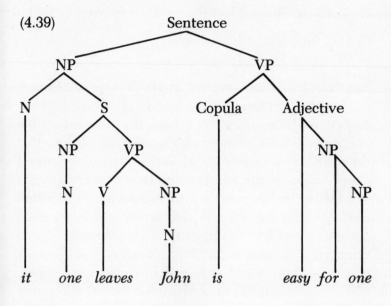

(4.40)

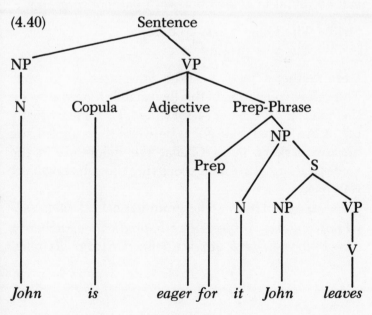

Note also the logical fact that (4.41) is implied by (4.35)

(4.41) One leaves John easily
(4.42) One leaves John eagerly

but that (4.42) is not implied by (4.36). This fact cannot be explained in terms of the surface structure of these sentences. Indeed, the superficial phrase markers for (4.35) and (4.36), namely (4.37), offer no clue to this difference in logical form. Moreover, no more refined classification of the constituents that appear in (4.37) will lead to a revision of their superficial phrase markers that can account for the difference in their logical consequences. For example, the most obvious of such attempts at a more refined classification, a division of adjectives into intentional and nonintentional types, will not do the trick, since the same logical difference can be found in connection with parallel cases like

(4.43) The sugar is easy to dissolve
(4.44) The sugar is slow to dissolve

Here neither adjective can be considered intentional. Thus, the explanation of this logical difference between the consequence set of (4.35) and (4.36) comes directly out of the formal differences between their underlying phrase markers, in particular, the difference in the configurations of symbols specifying the subject–object relations in each case.

As suggested above, the grammatical relations *subject-of-sentence, subject-of-verb, predicate-of-sentence, direct-object-of-verb*, etc., are defined in terms of configurations of symbols in phrase markers. In transformational theory, their definitions are restricted to configurations of symbols in underlying phrase markers. This restriction is imposed just to avoid such problems as are posed by cases like (4.35) and (4.36). Thus, for taxonomic description, there can be no uniform or generally acceptable way of defining grammatical relations because there are cases where the relevant configurations of symbols are the same in their superficial phrase markers and yet the grammatical relations are different in each. But, in transformational theory, the existence of deep structure allows us to put forth such natural definitions as[34]

(4.45)   (i) Subject-of-S = [NP,S]
         (ii) Predicate-of-S = [VP,S]
         (iii) Direct-Object-of-S = [NP,VP]
         (iv) Main-Verb-of-S = [V,VP]

where [B,A] is the function associated with a rule of the form $A \underline{\qquad} X$ (where B is a category and $X = YBZ$, for some Y, Z (possibly null)). Given an underlying phrase marker for the terminal string W, the substring U of W bears the grammatical relation R to the substring V of W if $R = [B,A]$ given that V is dominated by a node labeled A which directly dominates YBZ and U is dominated by this occurrence of B. Abstractly,

---

[34]Chomsky, *Aspects of the Theory of Syntax*, ch. 2, sec. 2.2.

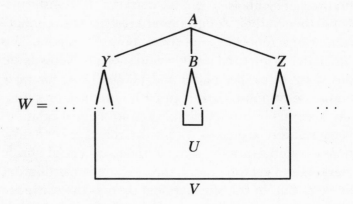

In terms of (4.45) (i)-(iv), we have

(4.46) (i) Subject-of-Verb = [[NP,S], [[V,VP] [VP,S]]

     (ii) Direct-Object-of-Verb = [[NP,VP], [V,VP]]

That is, x is the subject-of-the-verb y just in case x is the subject-of-a-sentence S and y is the main-verb-of-the-predicate-of-S, and z is-the-direct-object-of-the-verb y just in case z is the direct-object-of-a-verb-phrase whose main-verb is y.

By (4.46) in conjunction with (4.39), we can predict that "John" is the object of "leave" in (4.35); and, by (4.46) in conjunction with (4.40), we can predict that "John" is the subject of "leaves" in (4.36). These predictions are obviously correct, and the transformational rules that enable us to derive (4.37) from (4.39) and (4.40) offer a revealing explanation of the facts predicted. Finally, notice that (4.46) is the simplest generalization that explains the nature of the *subject-verb* and *verb-object* relations, since it extrapolates to complex cases like (4.35) and (4.36) the straightforward regularity found in simple cases like (4.38) and countless others.

Next consider the pair of sentences

(4.47)   I expected the doctor to examine John
(4.48)   I expected John to be examined by the doctor

They have the same meaning, for the verbal complement "John to be examined by the doctor" is just the passive form of the verbal complement "the doctor to examine John" in (4.47). This is to say that the relation between these verbal complements derives from the active-passive relation in

(4.49)   The doctor examined John
(4.50)   John was examined by the doctor.

But, from the viewpoint of the taxonomic theory, there is no difference between the pair (4.47) and (4.48) and the pair,

(4.51)   I persuaded the doctor to examine John
(4.52)   I persuaded John to be examined by the doctor

Yet (4.51) is obviously not a paraphrase of (4.52). Again, what cannot be explained at the level of surface structure can be easily explained if our analysis penetrates to the level of deep structure, for the underlying phrase marker of (4.47) and (4.48) is the same, *viz.*,

(4.53)

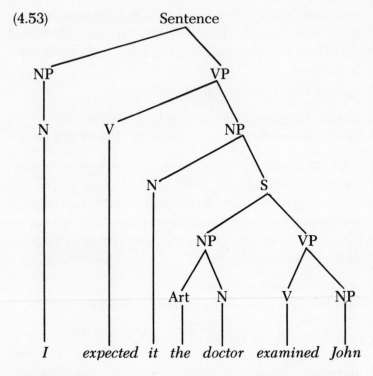

which by one route leads transformationally to the superficial phrase marker for (4.47) and by another to the superficial phrase marker for (4.48).[35] On the other hand, the underlying phrase markers for (4.51) and (4.52) are quite different in the relevant respects. The former is

[35] *Ibid.*, ch. 3.

(4.54)

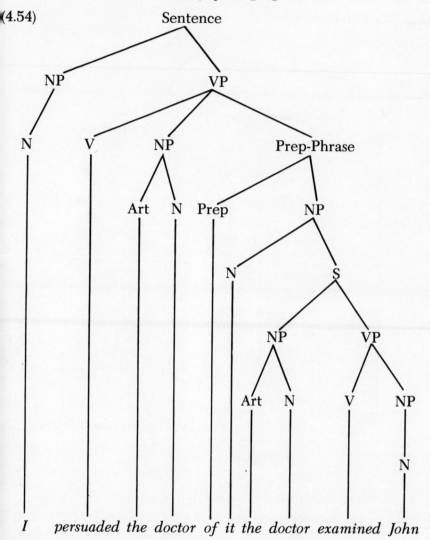

The latter is

(4.55)

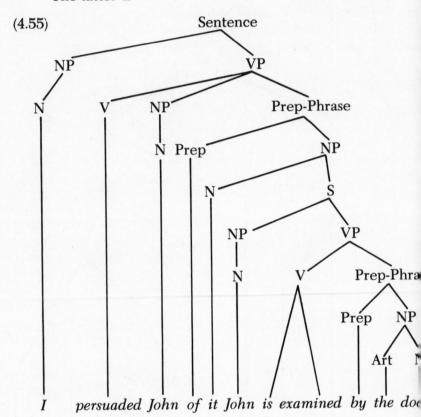

The transformations that map these underlying phrase markers into superficial phrase markers for (4.51) and (4.52), respectively, delete the subject of the embedded sentence structure (i.e., the subject of "examined") on the condition that it is identical with the object of the matrix sentence structure (i.e., the object of "persuade"), drop the preposition "of," and make other necessary formal adjustments.[36] It is quite clear, however, that (4.54) explains why in (4.51) we know it is the doctor whom the speaker has persuaded of something, and that (4.55) explains why in (4.52) we know it is John whom the speaker has persuaded of something. Thus transformational theory again predicts and explains significant facts that cannot be dealt with on taxonomic grounds.

Another type of case where the taxonomic theory fails is that in which one or more constituents are absent in the surface form of a sentence but are understood and are necessary for grammatical completeness. These cases are commonly called "ellipses." An example is

(4.56)   Turn the screw clockwise!

The surface form of the imperative does not contain a constituent that can be regarded as its subject, since a subject is defined as a noun phrase that occurs to the left of the verb in the verb phrase that is dominated by "Sentence" and the superficial structure of (4.56) is just:

---

[36]For a more detailed technical discussion, see P.S. Rosenbaum, *The Grammar of English Predicate Complement Constructions* (Cambridge: M.I.T. Press, 1967). For a much less detailed, but still somewhat technical discussion, cf. P.S. Rosenbaum, "Phrase Structure Principles of English Complex Sentence Formation," *Journal of Linguistics*, Vol. 3, No. 1, 103–118.

(4.57)

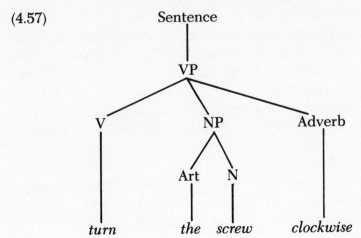

But a simple argument shows that (4.56) and other similar imperatives have a subject.

Reflexive pronouns occur in object position only when the noun whose pronoun representative is reflexivized, and the noun that occurs as subject of the sentence are identical. Thus the sentence

(4.58)   John defended himself

is grammatical but the sentences

(4.59)   John defended herself (itself, themselves, yourself)

are not. The underlying phrase marker for (4.58) is

(4.60)

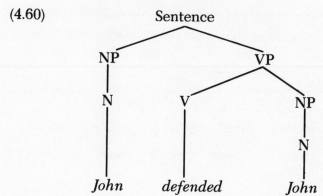

and the surface phrase marker for (4.58) is transformationally derived from (4.60) by reflexivization of the
object noun phrase on the basis of its identity with the
subject noun phrase (in the same simple sentence structure).

Actually, the subject and object noun phrases are
more abstractly represented than is indicated in (4.60).
In part, they are represented by a bundle of syntactic
features, such as [±Proper], [±Count], [±Human],
[±Masculine], etc. These feature symbols express the
properties with respect to which the identity or difference between the subject and the object noun phrases
is determined. Thus, the strings in (4.59) are not deriv-
able as well-formed sentences because there are no
underlying phrase markers in which the lexical item
"John" is marked [−Masculine] (and in the three other
cases [−Human], [−Singular], and [II-Person], respectively).

We note at this point that the only reflexive pronouns that can occur as the direct object in an imperative are "yourself" and "yourselves." That is to say, a sentence like (4.61) is grammatical

(4.61)   Turn yourself (yourselves) around!

but strings like those in (4.62) are ungrammatical

(4.62)   Turn himself (herself, itself, themselves) around!

and are ungrammatical for exactly the reasons that the strings in (4.59) are. From this we can draw the conclusion that imperative sentences like (4.56) and (4.61) must have a nominal subject that takes the form of the second person pronoun "you." Transformational grammars can easily incorporate this conclusion by allowing imperatives to come from 'NP+VP' structures, as in the underlying phrase markers:

(4.63)

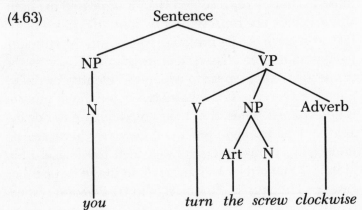

(4.64)

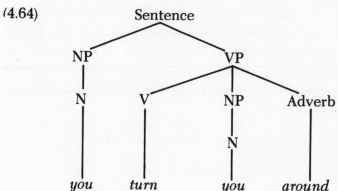

for the sentences (4.56) and (4.61), respectively. An optional transformation deletes "you" (and the branch connecting it to "Sentence") to produce the superficial phrase markers for cases like (4.56) and (4.61). The advantage of having this transformational rule optional is that cases like (4.61) will then have the same underlying phrase marker as cases like

(4.65)   You turn yourself around

and this fact will explain why they are paraphrases. Note also that on this hypothesis about the underlying reality of imperatives, it is possible to explain why they refer to the person addressed by the speaker. The taxonomic theory cannot handle any of these facts, insofar as there is no occurrence of "you" in the surface structure of these sentences.

Finally, let us consider a case of syntactic ambiguity that cannot be explained on the taxonomic theory. It will be recalled that the taxonomic theory can explain syntactic ambiguities such as are found in (4.13), since the same string of terminal symbols can be assigned different bracketings by rewriting rules alone, as with (4.14) and (4.15). But the ambiguity in

(4.66)   John knows a kinder person than Bill

is not reflected in its surface structure, since the constituents which disambiguate (4.66) and occur in

(4.67)   John knows a kinder person than Bill knows

and

(4.68)   John knows a kinder person than Bill is

are eliminated by ellipsis in (4.66). Since the ambiguity of (4.66). does not reside in the different ways in which certain elements in the string of terminal symbols are associated with each other, alternative segmentation and classification of (4.66) could not account for this ambiguity. Consequently, a taxonomic grammar will fail to predict and explain this type of ambiguity.

On the other hand, a transformational grammar, because it assigns both an underlying and a superficial phrase marker to a sentence, can treat a case such as (4.66) as one where two different deep structures collapse into one surface structure, and can use ellipsis to explain the source of the ambiguity. The explanation in a transformational grammar of English would thus be in terms of two underlying phrase markers that both have the "superstructure":

(4.69)

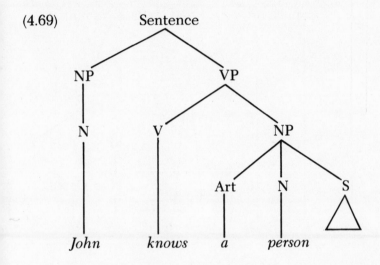

but differ in that $\overset{S}{\triangle}$ is different in each. In the underlying phrase marker for (4.66) on which its interpretation as fully synonymous with (4.68) depends, $\overset{S}{\triangle}$ is:

(4.70)

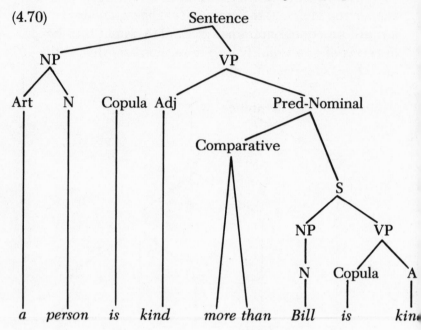

In the transformational development of (4.70) the repetition of "is kind" is deleted, giving the string "a person is kind more than Bill," and then "more" attaches to the adjective "kind" in the form "er," giving the string "a person kinder than Bill." Then, by (4.26) (R1) and (R2), we obtain the string "John knows a person who is kinder than Bill," and by (4.26) (R4) we obtain (4.66). The fact that (4.66) is a paraphrase of (4.68) can be explained because (4.69), in which $\underset{\triangle}{S}$ is (4.70), is also the underlying phrase marker for (4.68). We obtain (4.68) just as we obtained (4.66) except that instead of deleting both the repeated copula and adjective "is kind" we

only delete the adjective "kind." On the other hand, in
the underlying phrase marker for (4.66) on which its
interpretation as fully synonymous with (4.67) depends,
$\overset{S}{\triangle}$ is:

71)

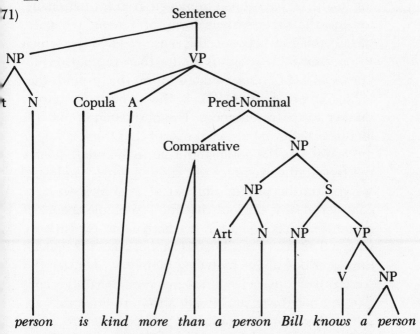

In the transformational development from (4.69),
where $\overset{S}{\triangle}$ is (4.71), to the superficial phrase marker for
(4.67), we run through the strings:

John knows a person a person is kind more than a person Bill knows,
John knows a person a person is kind more than Bill knows
John knows a person a person is kinder than Bill knows
John knows a person who is kinder than Bill knows
John knows a kinder person than Bill knows
John knows a kinder person than Bill.

Therefore, the ambiguity in (4.66) is explained on the assumption that the conflicting interpretations do not come directly from the surface form of (4.66), but rather come from underlying forms whose differentiating features have been removed transformationally, leaving the same surface form. Moreover, the paraphrase relation between the sense of (4.66) on which the person John knows is kinder than the person Bill knows and (4.67) is accounted for on the grounds that (4.69), where $\overset{S}{\triangle}$ is (4.71), is the underlying phrase marker for both sentences. The derivation of (4.67) is identical with that of (4.66) except that the last step is not taken, i.e., the optional transformation that deletes the repeated occurrence of "knows" is not employed.

Even on the limited number of examples we have considered, it is obvious that the taxonomic theory of grammar is inadequate in predictive and explanatory power. The taxonomic linguist cannot meet the difficulties described above by trying somehow to enrich the structure of superficial phrase markers so that they contain the necessary constituent structure otherwise absent in these representations of surface structure. More elaborate segmentation and classification cannot overcome the inherent inability of taxonomic description to deal with grammatical relations, ellipsis, and other aspects of the relation between deep and surface structure. Such attempts to meet these difficulties would not only be *ad hoc* but would immediately lead to false predictions about the phonetic shape of sentences. Tampering with the single phrase marker assigned to a sentence in a taxonomic description produces modifications of the superficial phrase marker that imply incorrect characterizations of surface similarities (like those between (4.47) and (4.48), on the one hand, and (4.51) and (4.52), on the other; or between (4.35) and (4.36)) and surface differences (like that between (4.61) and (4.65)). The superficial phrase marker has its proper role to play in syntactic description: It must provide the surface structure information which is required by the phonological component to determine the phonetic shape of the sentence. What is wrong with taxonomic theory is that the superficial phrase marker is the only syntactic description of a sentence sanctioned in the theory. Thus, either it cannot carry information about deep structure or else it cannot play its proper role for the phonological component. Therefore, the transformationalist claim about the existence of an underlying level of syntactic structure has to be accepted as the obvious and natural way out of this dilemma.

5.
The Underlying Semantic Reality of Language

⸺⟨∞⟩⸺

Theory construction has proceeded far enough in the areas of syntax and phonology, and has become familiar enough, at least in general terms, for the non-specialist to have a fairly clear idea of these subjects. In semantics, however, the situation is different. Theory construction has not gone very far, and many conflicting proposals exist concerning the meaning of 'meaning'. Chomsky once observed, " 'Meaning' tends to be used as a catch-all term to include every aspect of language that we know very little about."[37] The problem is that there are too many "theories," each talking about something different and none sufficiently articulate to make clear to what aspect of language it is addressed. So, instead of having a semantic theory to which we can appeal for clarification of the subject, we must seek clarification first in order to get a theory.

The big question of semantics is "What is meaning?"

---

[37]N. Chomsky, *Syntactic Structures*, pp. 103–104.

But *how* do we go about trying to answer so big a question? In the past, linguists, philosophers, and psychologists have attempted to answer this question directly. We find, historically, a variety of direct answers. These include the Plantonic answer that meanings are eternal archetypes; the Lockean answer that meanings are the mental ideas for which words stand as external signs; the answer that meanings are the things in the world to which words refer; the Wittgensteinian answer that meaning is use; the behaviorist answer that meanings are the stimuli that elicit verbal responses; the introspectionalist answer that meanings are mental images associated with verbal behavior; and so on. But every attempt to give a direct answer has failed. Some, such as the Platonic answer, proved too vague and speculative. Others gave the wrong results. For example, consider the doctrine that the meaning of a word is the image in the minds of the speaker and hearer accompanying its use. This doctrine gives the wrong account of the distinction between meaningful and meaningless expressions. Words like "possibility," "randomness," "chance," "therefore," "ineffability," etc., are falsely predicted to be meaningless, while expressions like Lewis Carroll's "slithy toves" count as meaningful.

Three attempts to provide a direct answer to the question "What is meaning?" are of special interest for us because they constitute an attempt to give a non-Democritean theory of semantic structure. These three "direct answers" are the *referential theory*, the *stimulus–response theory*, and the *use theory*. Each

identifies the meaning of a sentence or constituent
with some external, publically observable object,
event, act, etc. Their attractiveness to taxonomic linguists thus lies in the fact that they each provide an
hypothesis about meaning which is consistent with taxonomic theory because these hypotheses do not require
that the semantic structure of a sentence be a part of
its grammatical structure.

The referential theory identifies the meaning of an
expression with the actual entity, class of entities,
event, or class of events that the expression names,
refers to, denotes, designates, or stands for. Accordingly, the meaning of "Bertrand Russell" is the man
named by this proper noun; the meaning of "men"
is the class of adult male human beings (including Bertrand Russell, Attila, each John Smith, etc.); the meaning of "Columbus' discovery of America" is the
historical event of 1492; and the meaning of "birth" is
the class of events, each of which initiates the independent life of an animal or human. But this theory does
not stand up. If the theory were true, then every expression that refers to the same thing(s) would be the
same in meaning. Since not all such expressions are
synonymous, the theory is false. One counter-example
is Frege's case of the expressions "the morning star"
and "the evening star," both of which refer to the same
object, the planet Venus, but which clearly differ in
meaning in the way that the terms "evening" and
"morning" do.[38] We can perhaps better appreciate this

[38]G. Frege, "On Sense and Reference," in *Translations from the Philosophical Writings of Gottlob Frege*, pp. 56–78.

semantic difference if we note with Frege that the discovery that the evening star is the morning star was an
achievement of empirical astronomy, not an achievement of lexicography or semantics. This point can be
restated: "Sir Walter Scott" and "the author of *Waverley*," name the same Scottish novelist. If these expressions were the same in meaning, as are "ophthalmologist" and "physician specializing in defects and
diseases of the eye," then the truth of the sentence "Sir
Walter Scott is the author of *Waverley*" would be entirely a linguistic affair, as is the case with the sentence
"An ophthalmologist is a physician specializing in defects and diseases of the eye." But, since the truth of the
former is an historical rather than a linguistic matter,
we have another case where sameness of reference
does not coincide with sameness of meaning. Another
such counterexample against the referential theory
comes from the fact that words that refer to nothing at
all, e.g., "unicorn," "witch," "warlock," are required,
on this theory, to be synonymous, which they are not.
From this evidence, we can conclude that the theory is
false because sameness of reference is not a sufficient
condition for synonymy.[39]

The stimulus-response theory has dominated modern

[39]This "naive version" of the referential theory has been abandoned by
every serious philosopher, and abandoned with such quick disdain and finality that there has only been one direct attempt to salvage referential theories by formulating them in a more sophisticated way. This attempt was
made in N. Goodman, "On Likeness of Meaning," *Semantics and the Philosophy of Language*, L. Linsky, ed. (Urbana: University of Illinois Press, 1952),
pp. 66–74. The attempt fails, however, cf. J.J. Katz, *Semantic Theory*, ch. 6.

psychology and has had a strong following in modern philosophy[40] and linguistics. Bloomfield, who was the major figure in twentieth-century taxonomic linguistics, claimed that the meaning of an utterance or linguistic form can be defined as

> the situation in which the speaker utters it and the response which it calls forth in the hearer. The speaker's situation and the hearer's response are closely coordinated, thanks to the circumstance that every one of us learns to act indifferently as a speaker or as a hearer. In the causal sequence, speaker's situation—speech—hearer's response, the speaker's situation will usually present a simpler aspect than the hearer's response; therefore we usually discuss and define meanings in terms of a speaker's stimulus.[41]

Meaning, then, is the causally effective or precipitating components of a situation, those which prompt the speaker to verbalization. Thus the stimuli which elicit an utterance constitute its meaning. Sometimes the notion of stimuli is used as a circumlocution for the notion of that to which a linguistic form refers. For example, Bloomfield says that

> it is clear that we must discriminate between *non-distinctive* features of the situation, such as the size, shape, color, and so on of any one particular apple, and the *distinctive*, or *linguistic meaning* (the *semantic* features) which are common to all the situations that call forth the utterance of the linguistic form, such as the

---

[40]For example, W.V. Quine, *Word and Object*, ch. II.
[41]L. Bloomfield, *Language* (New York: Holt, 1933), p. 139.

features which are common to all the objects of which English-speaking people use the word *apple*.[42]

But in such cases the stimulus-response theory of meaning becomes identical to the referential theory and must, therefore, break down for the same reasons. Consequently, we should consider this theory independent of qualifications that identify it with the referential theory in order to give it a run for its money.

By some curious irony, it sometimes happens that the proponent of a theory, in presenting it, will cite just the type of case that leads to its refutation. Bloomfield writes,

> People very often utter a word like *apple* when no apple at all is present. We may call this *displaced speech*. The frequency and importance of displaced speech is obvious. We recall the infant "asking for" his doll.[43]

Calling this case "displaced speech," with the implication that that will keep it from being a counterexample to the theory, is exactly like defending the theory that everyone is a genius by labeling any case of lower intelligence "displaced brains."

Other stimulus-response theorists, especially in psychology,[44] have sought to avoid this difficulty by saying that the meaning of an utterance is the stimulus whose

---

[42] *Ibid.*, p. 141.
[43] *Ibid.*
[44] For example, B.F. Skinner, *Verbal Behavior* (New York: Appleton-Century-Crofts, 1957).

presentation increases the probability of the utterance's occurrence. But though this does avoid the particular counterexample—since the theory, as now formulated, no longer requires that the stimulus identified as the meaning of an utterance be the cause that elicits it—the very fact about natural languages that gives rise to this counterexample also brings about the downfall of this reformulated version. For the fact in question is that the use of natural languages is, in general, free from the control of external stimuli in the speech-situation. The presence of such stimuli cannot possibly increase the probability that a speaker in the situation will utter a given sentence, for, as we observed earlier, the sentence he utters will almost always be new; and since the probability of an event is determined by the relative frequency with which it has occurred in the past, the probability of a given new sentence occurring at a given time and place is certainly zero.[45] It is, in fact, just this freedom from stimulus control that makes natural languages suitable for expressing the products of creative thought. No doubt there are cases where a speaker's utterance is under the control of local stimuli so that such stimuli, together with the speaker's recent history of deprivation, punishment, and reward, provide some probability that he will utter a certain sentence, for example, the case of the man whose arm is being painfully twisted by a bully

---

[45]As indicated in footnote 23, in the normal employment of a natural language, the sentences which occur are characteristically new ones. Repetitions occur rarely, mainly in cases of habitual greetings, such as "How do you do?," clichés, and so forth.

who tells him he must say "uncle" before he will release him. But of course such cases, which are the only ones that fit the stimulus-response theory, are extremely rare and highly atypical.

That freedom from stimulus control is a necessary condition for any language that is to serve as a vehicle for communicating whatever might come into the mind of a speaker is a point that deserves added emphasis. Suppose we are shown a painting during a visit to an art gallery. We might come out with almost anything, e.g., "That is a painting," "*That* is a painting?," "Ugly," "I can't think of anything witty to say," "Can you let me have an aspirin?," "Let's try to get our admission fee back," "The answer to the riddle you told me yesterday just occurred to me," "My thoughts just keep rambling," and so on, *ad infinitum*. Since whatever ends a train of thought can be readily expressed in language, stimulus control implies strict control of our thought processes by local stimuli. Moreover, if what we say were really under stimulus control, as this theory claims, we would go around uttering "air" all the time, but, in fact, the utterance "air" rarely occurs except as a gasp when air is absent.

Psychologists like Skinner[46] who adopt this theory of meaning define "stimulus" and "response" as (respectively) a component of the local situation and a piece of overt behavior that are lawfully related to each other by smooth, reproducible curves on the basis of which the latter can be predicted from the former. In the face

[46]B. F. Skinner, *Verbal Behavior*.

of obvious, contravening facts like those cited in the immediately preceding paragraph, such psychologists can only reply that each of these verbal responses is under the control of different properties of the stimulus painting. To this sort of reply, Chomsky has remarked:

> This device is as simple as it is empty. Since properties are free for the asking, . . . we can account for a wide class of responses in terms of Skinnerian functional analysis by identifying the *controlling stimuli*. But the word *stimulus* has lost all objectivity in this usage. Stimuli are no long part of the outside physical world; they are driven back into the organism. We identify the stimulus when we hear the response. It is clear from such examples, which abound, that the talk of *stimulus control* simply disguises a complete retreat to mentalistic psychology.[47]

This is well taken. We are in no position to predict the speaker's response until it occurs and we can infer from it what he was responding to. When a man looks at a painting and says, "The answer to the riddle you told me yesterday just occurred to me," we do not even know how far back in time we must extend our notion of the stimulus-situation until we hear the response. Moreover, if we extend the situation back far enough so that it includes the verbalization which acquainted the speaker with the riddle, the only property of this stimulus that is in any sense related to his utterance is

[47]N. Chomsky, "A Review of B.F. Skinner's *Verbal Behavior*," reprinted in *The Structure of Language: Readings in the Philosophy of Language*, p. 553.

simply that it is what he is thinking about while looking at the painting. Thus Chomsky is quite right: Such properties are not external physical properties but "old-fashioned" mental ones.

Another non-Democritean theory of meaning is the doctrine that meaning is use. This is the view that Wittgenstein came to adopt as a solution to the dilemma he thought he was in, in having to choose between a traditional, Platonistic conception of logical form and a "dead" formalist alternative (cf. Chapter 2 of this monograph). The doctrine is that the meaning of a sentence or constituent is the use that speakers of the language make of it in carrying on social intercourse. The difficulty with this doctrine is that meaning is only *one* factor that contributes to the ways linguistic constructions are used. There are many others, so that an explication of meaning in terms of use is bound to falsely represent semantic relations in cases where non-semantic factors contribute to differences in use. For example, there are synonymous words like "bunny" and "rabbit," "piggy" and "pig," "stomach" and "tummy," etc., that have different conditions of use because of certain social conventions that have nothing whatever to do with meaning. "Bunny" and "piggy" are used appropriately when the speaker is himself a child or when he is speaking to a child. "Rabbit" and "pig," although, respectively, the same in meaning, have no such condition on their use. Another example is the strictures against using "four-letter words" in polite society that do not carry over to their scientific-sounding synonyms. Still another example is the

obvious difference in use between a simple sentence
like "A man walked up some stairs" and a prolix, synonymous sentence like "A male member of the human
race covered the distance from the bottom to the top
of a flight of steps, arranged in series for ascending or
descending, on foot, without running, and moving by
steps such that one of his feet was not lifted entirely
before the other touched down."

The failure of attempts to provide a direct answer to
the question "What is meaning?" has resulted in semantics itself gaining the undeserved reputation of being
an irretrievably dreary discipline, where nothing can
be established with any degree of finality. But it is not
semantics, but rather approaches to semantics that in-
sist on a direct answer to the question "What is meaning?" at the very outset, that deserve this unsavory
reputation. Imagine what would have happened if
ancient astronomers had insisted on knowing what
sorts of things planets are before trying to describe
their movements. Or, better yet, suppose mathemati-
cians had insisted on a direct answer to the question
"What are numbers?" before trying to explain arithmetic properties and relations like 'is the sum of', 'is the
square root of', and 'is a prime number'. We would now
be without a theory of arithmetic (i.e., number theory).

Therefore, I propose to adopt an approach which is
the opposite of the one followed in the past. I will try
to answer the big question of semantics by *not* trying to answer it.[48]

[48]The theory of meaning to be sketched below is set forth in detail in my
book *Semantic Theory*. It was first presented in J.J. Katz and J.A. Fodor,
"The Structure of a Semantic Theory," *Language*, vol. 39, No. 2 (Part 1),

This is not as paradoxical as it first sounds. Generally in science one begins an inquiry by breaking down big questions into little ones, which are more specific and thus more manageable, but which are still components of the big question. Such smaller, more modest questions tell us what properties and relations comprise our subject matter and so set guidelines for theory construction. Therefore, they provide us with the necessary pretheoretic conception of our subject from which theory construction begins.

Accordingly, we ought to try to break down "What is meaning?" into a number of smaller, more modest questions, the answer to each of which is a part of the answer to the big question. Proceeding in this way, we obtain the following sample of questions about semantic properties and relations:

(5.1) What is the difference between meaningfulness and meaninglessness?

(5.2) What is sameness of meaning? What is the difference between synonymy and nonsynonymy?

(5.3) What is multiplicity of meaning or ambiguity?

(5.4) What is truth by virtue of meaning and what is falsehood by virtue of meaning?

(5.5) What is semantic redundancy?

(5.6) What is entailment by virtue of meaning?

(April-June 1963), 170–210. The first chapter of *Semantic Theory*, the article "The Structure of a Semantic Theory," and the sketch in this monograph present somewhat different introductions to the kind of theory I wish to construct, so that the former two should be looked at by someone who desires further perspective.

(5.7)   What is presupposition?

(5.8)   What is superordination?

(5.9)   What is incompatibility of meaning?

(5.10) What is a self-answered question?

The semantic properties and relations asked about in these questions may be illustrated by some examples. The contrast between meaningfulness and meaninglessness is seen in comparing "Open jars empty quickly" with "Waterproof shadows empty foolishly." The contrast between sameness and difference of meaning is seen in comparing the synonymous expressions "my sister" and "a female offspring of my parents other than myself" with the nonsynonymous expressions "my brother" and "a broken chair in my attic." Ambiguity is illustrated by the example "I took the photo," which, among other things, means that the speaker photographed something and that he stole a photograph. "Uncles are male" is true by virtue of its meaning and "Aunts are male" is false by virtue of its meaning. Semantic redundancy is exhibited by the expression "naked nude." The sentence "Monarchs are anachronistic" entails the sentence "Kings are anachronistic": The inference from the former to the latter is justified by their meaning alone. The question asked by the interrogative "When did you stop beating your wife?" presupposes that the person addressed has been beating his wife but has stopped the practice. The superordination relation is exhibited by such pairs of words as "finger" and "thumb," "tree" and "oak," and "dwelling" and "cottage." The meanings of the words in the pairs "open" and "close," "whisper" and "shout," and "boy" and "girl" are incompatible. Finally, interrogatives like "Is breakfast a meal?" and "What is the color of a red car?" provide their own answers.

Taken together, these semantic properties and relations provide a reasonably good initial conception of the subject matter of semantics. They circumscribe an area of grammatical phenomena, beyond both phonology and syntax, for which a theory is needed, even though the properties and relations asked about in questions (5.1)-(5.10) represent only a sample, perhaps even a small one, of the full range of those with which semantics must ultimately deal. Semantic theory, we may now say, explains the nature of these properties and relations, and any others to which its principles extend. Ultimately, we will say that the full domain of semantics contains just the phenomena embraced by semantic theory.

Thus, we will proceed by concentrating on trying to answer the smaller, more manageable questions of semantics. Once a theory has been built that successfully answers a reasonably large number of them, we may tackle the big question. Then we can base our answer to "What is meaning?" on what our theory had to assume about meaning in order to provide explanations of this reasonably large number of semantic properties and relations. This approach will be in the spirit of the one used by astronomers to discover the nature of the planets. Astronomers discovered that the planets are physical objects by first developing the theory that the movements of the planets obey standard mechanical laws.

How, then, do we begin to frame a theory that will explain semantic properties and relations? Again, I suggest we take our cue from science.

Historians of science often tell us that sciences begin with commonsense reflection and proceed by systematic reformulations to highly abstract theories. Commonsense reflection about language tells us that what makes an expression or sentence ambiguous is that it has more than one sense, that what makes an expression or sentence meaningful is that it has a sense, that what makes one meaningless is that it does not have a sense, that what makes two expressions or sentences synonymous is that they have a sense in common, and that what makes a modifier redundant is that its sense is already contained in the sense of the head with which it is in construction. To proceed from these commonsense definitions to a theory that explains the nature of ambiguity, meaningfulness, synonymy, redundancy, etc., we must find some way to formally reconstruct such definitions within the theory of grammar.

To determine how to formalize them, let us see how the theory of grammar discussed above already formalizes corresponding syntactic properties and relations. A generative grammar has a level of syntactic representation at which the organization of sentences is described by phrase markers, whose non-terminal portion represents the "positions" which morphemes, words, phrases, and clauses can occupy and whose terminal portion represents assignments of sentential constituents to such "positions." The common sense definition of the relation, '*x* is the same part of speech as *y*', as understood in conventional school grammar, means that *x* and *y* can, in general, occupy the same positions in sentences. This relation can be formally defined over underlying phrase markers by the following:

(5.11)   *x* is the same part of speech as *y* if, and only if, for any phrase markers M_i and M_j (not necessarily distinct) in which *x* and *y* occur, *x* and *y* are dominated by nodes bearing the same major-category label (e.g., 'Noun', 'Verb', etc.) in M_i and M_j.

We note two aspects of this formalization. First, since the phrase markers of a sentence represent its syntactic structure, the definition says that constituents belong to the same part of speech category by virtue of their syntactic form. Second, the defining condition is formal because the phrase markers to which it refers are formal. Accordingly, since an expression or sentence has a certain semantic property or bears a certain semantic relation to another by virtue of its meaning, we might reasonably try to give the definitions of semantic properties and relations in terms of representations of meaning that, like phrase markers, are formal objects generated by the grammar.

So, the desire for formal reconstructions of common sense definitions of semantic properties and relations leads us to set up a level of semantic representation in grammars on which there will be formal objects whose structure can be utilized to define semantic properties and relations in the way that the structure of phrase markers is used to define syntactic relations like 'x is the same part of speech as y'. That is, we are led to set up a semantic level of representation in order to replace *in*formal definitions like "x and y have a sense in common" by formal ones in the way that informal definitions in syntax like "x and y occupy the same positions in sentences" are replaced by formal ones like (5.11).

The initial step in setting up such a level is to find some means of representing the senses of words formally. As a first guess, we might say that a sense of a morpheme or lexical item is represented by a single formal symbol and that different senses of the same or other lexical item(s) are represented by distinct formal symbols. But this hypothesis is easily proven wrong. Semantically redundant expressions like "male boy," "female aunt," "unmarried bachelor," etc., show that we cannot take the sense of a lexical item to be an undifferentiated, monolithic whole, as is assumed by representing it with a single symbol. The proper generalization about these redundancies is that the whole of the sense of the modifier is included as part of the sense of its head. To express this generalization, we shall at least have to analyze the sense of nouns such as "boy," "aunt," and "bachelor" into the component which is identical to the sense of such a modifier and the component which is different. Therefore, single symbols in semantic representation must stand for parts of senses, or as we shall say, *concepts* out of which senses are formed. If we carry the analysis of the composition of sense to its logical conclusion, the semantic representation of senses, both of lexical items and syntactically complex constituents, will be composed of a configuration of single symbols, each of which stands for an atomic concept. These symbols will be referred to as *primitive semantic markers.* These together with representations of concepts defined in terms of them will be referred to as *semantic markers.*

We cannot be expected to set forth the primitive semantic markers in the way that a logician sets forth the primitives of a formalized language. As Frege once observed, ". . . something logically simple is no more given us at the outset than most of the chemical elements are; it is reached only by means of scientific work." We eventually hope to reach the semantic simples of natural language, by making semantic representation richer and richer in structure, so that it can explain the semantic properties and relations of more and more sentences. But, for the time being, we have to present the semantic representations of lexical items in terms of semantic markers. In doing so, however, we make no assumption about the final status of these semantic markers in the vocabulary of semantic theory.

Accordingly, we might represent one sense of the word "bachelor" by the set of semantic markers:

(5.12)   (Object), (Physical), (Human), (Adult), (Male), (Not married)

Our linguistic intuitions that "unmarried bachelor" is semantically redundant and that "He is a bachelor again" is not semantically anomalous tell us that one component of this sense of "bachelor" is the concept of being in an unmarried state. Our linguistic intuition that "aunt," "sister," "mother," "spinster," etc., differ semantically from "uncle," "brother," "father," "bachelor," etc., only with respect to the conceptual distinction between femaleness and maleness tells us that another component of the sense of "bachelor" is the concept of maleness. Our linguistic intuition that "John is a bachelor" entails "John is human" tells us that still another component of the sense of "bachelor" is the concept of humanness. Finally, our linguistic intuition that the sentence "The bachelor fell from the 53rd floor and broke both himself and the pavement when he landed" is meaningful whereas the sentence "The shadow (reflection, after-image, etc.) fell from the 53rd floor and broke both itself and the pavement when it landed" is semantically deviant tells us that still another conceptual component of the sense of "bachelor" is the concept of being a physical object (as opposed to a perceptual object).

A set of semantic markers that functions as the semantic representation of a sense of a constituent is called a *reading.* We distinguish between *lexical readings* and *derived readings,* depending on whether the reading is assigned to a lexical item (a syntactically minimal unit) or to a syntactically complex constituent. Since there are only finitely many lexical items in the grammar, we can list an appropriate set of lexical readings for each lexical item that occurs in the lexicon component of the syntactic component (cf. (4.24) and (4.25)). We can refer to such a mapping of lexical readings onto lexical items as a *dictionary*.

How is the semantic component of the grammar to assign derived readings to syntactically complex constituents as representations of their senses? Semanticists must not only represent the meaning of syntactic atoms like "boy," "a," "run," "the," "under," "short," etc., but also the meaning of the syntactically complex expressions and sentences, like

(5.13)   (i) The short run of the short boy
         (ii) the boy ran under a short boy

which the syntactic rules can construct out of such atoms. Complex expressions and sentences, after all, exhibit the same range of semantic properties and relations as syntactic atoms. But, what is more important, from the point of the speaker's ability to produce and understand novel sentences, the speaker's semantic competence is more a question of what he can do with the dictionary information he has than of the dictionary information itself. Here, however, we cannot simply list each case and assign it a reading. Syntactic rules generate complex expressions, and hence sentences, by a process that can go on infinitely. That is, it is, in principle, always possible to continue a sentence, no matter how long it already is, and thereby form a still longer one. Since there is no longest expression or sentence, nor a most complex one, there is no possibility of listing cases one by one, as is done in a dictionary. By the same token, the semantic competence of a speaker cannot consist of a list of the meanings of the words, phrases, clauses, and sentences of his language. For while the speaker's storage capacity is finite, his ability to comprehend meanings, apart from such irrelevant performance restrictions as the finitude of his life span, his memory limitations, etc., extends over the infinite set of sentences generated in the grammar. What we want to find out, therefore, is what sort of internalized principles enable a speaker to obtain infinitely many meanings on a finite basis. Given some notion as to the nature of these principles, we can formulate rules of the semantic component as their explicit formalizations.

Here we can avail ourselves of a traditional principle of semantics, namely, the principle of compositionality. This principle says that the meaning of a syntactically complex constituent, from words to sentences, is a compositional function of the meanings of its parts. This is an initially plausible account of the speaker's internalized principles because unless some such mechanism is part of the linguistic competence of the speakers of a language it would be impossible to explain how they are able, in principle, to produce and understand infinitely many sentences, given that the storage capability of their brains is finite. But if we assume such a principle to be part of their internalized competence, we can explain this fact by supposing that they store only the meanings of the finitely many lexical items of their language and obtain the meanings of the constructions formed out of these lexical items by using the compositional principle. Moreover, idioms, such as "shoot the breeze," "stir up trouble," "give hell to," etc., which are the only exceptions to compositionality, are exceptions that prove the rule. Unless the rest of the language were compositional, idioms could not be correctly defined as the cases where the sense of the whole is not a function of the senses of its parts.

To obtain a representation of the meanings of sentences compositionally from the meanings of their smallest syntactic parts, we require both a *dictionary* and a *projection rule*. The projection rule specifies how lexical readings for the syntactic atoms of a complex expression or sentence can be combined to form derived readings for the whole expression or sentence which explain its compositional meaning.

First, as a finite basis from which representations of the meanings of infinitely many complex constituents can be projected, the semantic component will have to have a dictionary in which an entry occurs for each noncomplex constituent in the language, i.e., for each lexical item. Second, it will have to have a projection rule, which can be regarded as the formal analogue of the speaker's compositional principles and which constitute the combinatorial machinery for projecting representations of the meanings of complex constituents from this finite basis. The entries in the dictionary are formal representations of the meanings of the lexical items, and the projection rules generate formal representations of the meanings of complex constituents from the formal representations of the meanings of their component lexical items.

Two things are presupposed here. First, that the pro-

jection rule will receive an account of all the constituents that make up a sentence, and second, that it will
be told what the grammatical relations between these
constituents are. Clearly, the projection rule cannot be
expected to get a representation of the meaning of a
sentence from representations of the meanings of its
constituents if it is not provided with a full enumeration
of such constituents. And since the same constituents in
different grammatical relations to one another can
mean different things, as for instance in

(5.14)   John thought he had left Mary alone
(5.15)   Mary alone thought he had left John
(5.16)   Had he alone thought Mary left John

the projection rule must be provided with a full statement of such relations.

At this point we find a remarkable coincidence between what the semantic component demands and
what the syntactic component supplies. The phrase
markers generated by the base rules of the syntactic
component in Chomsky's theory of syntax, the phrase
markers that represent deep syntactic structure, seem
to supply exactly the information required by the projection rule. These underlying phrase markers specify
all the constituents of a sentence and their grammatical
relations. Therefore, by having the dictionary and the
projection rule apply to the underlying phrase markers
we satisfy both of the demands of the semantic component.

Thus, the process of forming and assigning semantic
representations will work as follows. The underlying

phrase marker(s) of a sentence will be input to the semantic component of a grammar, which is composed of a dictionary and a projection rule. First, the dictionary will assign a set of lexical readings to each lexical item of the sentence, by associating each terminal symbol of an underlying phrase marker with just those lexical readings from its dictionary entry that are compatible with its syntactic description in the phrase marker. Second, the projection rule will combine lexical readings, then the derived readings that result from such combinations, and so on, until a set of readings is associated with each constituent of the sentence, including the whole sentence itself. These combinations will be made only in case constituents are gramatically related. The type of combination is determined by the type of grammatical relation obtaining between the constituents whose readings are to be combined.

This process of combination must also weed out readings. If we count the number of senses that the lexical items of an ordinary fifteen- or twenty-word sentence has and compute the number of possible combinations that can be formed from them when they are paired up in accord with the grammatical relations of the sentence, the number of possible senses of the sentence runs into the hundreds. Since no sentence of a natural language has anywhere near this number of senses, and some have none at all, there must be a rather severe form of selection going on in the process of producing derived readings.

The fact that some sentences have no sense, even though their individual words are meaningful, e.g.,

(5.17)   Shadows are waterproof

indicates that meaninglessness, the absence of any sense, is the limit of the same selectional process that gives rise to ambiguity. To put the point another way: Degree of ambiguity, from one sense (zero degree) to any number of senses less than the total possible on the basis of the available combinations of lexical senses, is the case where the selectional process stops short of the limit. This indicates that the reconstruction of selection can be based on the kind of semantic irregularities that produce meaningless sentences.

Here we can make use of some traditional ideas about meaninglessness from philosophy. Since Aristotle, it has been recognized that concepts fall into categories and that the category of a concept specifies the other concepts with which it can combine to assert something of some object in its range of predication. Thus, if, by virtue of the flexibility of syntax, a concept is combined with one outside its category, the sentence which puts them into combination will be conceptually absurd, or meaningless, as in the case of (5.17). Hence, to reconstruct such selection, we have to build this notion of category into the representations of lexical senses.

Saying that something is waterproof means that water cannot pass through its surface to the inside. Since a surface is the exterior of a physical object, the concept of a physical object is the category of the concept waterproof. Thus, being waterproof can be attributed to things like coats, cars, and cigarettes, that fall under the concept physical object, but not to things like after-images, reflections, and shadows, that do not. Now, the category in which an object must fall in order for a concept to be predicated of it will appear among the concepts in the definition of the word that refers to the object, e.g., the concept *physical object* appears among the concepts that define "coat" (i.e., the concepts *physical object, artifact, outer garment, fits the upper part of the body* define "coat"). Therefore, it will be natural to reconstruct the selectional feature that prevents (5.17) from receiving a sense by requiring that nouns modified by "waterproof" have the semantic marker (physical object) in their reading. If this semantic marker is absent, the reading of "waterproof" cannot combine with the reading of its nominal head to form a reading for the higher constituent of which this adjective and this nominal head are parts. Thus, the requirement is to be formulated within the lexical reading of the adjective "waterproof" and stated as a restriction on the class of senses with which the sense of "waterproof" can combine to form others.

These requirements we call *selection restrictions*. They are found in almost all lexical readings. We may also think of this feature of a lexical reading as reconstructing the different ranges of application of the different senses of the same lexical item. For example, the word "handsome" has one sense where it means something like "beautiful with dignity," another where it means something like "gracious or generous," and still another where it means something like "moderately large." The first of these senses applies to persons and artifacts, the second to conduct, and the third to amounts. Therefore, the expressions "handsome man," "handsome introduction," and "handsome loan" differ appropriately in meaning. For example, the first of the three senses of "handsome" would be represented by a reading with a selection restriction of the form $< \text{(Human)}_i \overline{V}_i \text{(Artifact)} >$, the second by one with a selection restriction of the form $< \text{(Conduct)} >$, and the third by one with a selection restriction of the form $< \text{(Amount)} >$. The first can combine only with readings that contain either the semantic marker (Human) or (Artifact), the second only with readings that contain (Conduct), and the third only with readings that contain (Amount). Thus because the reading of "desk" contains the semantic marker (Artifact) but not (Conduct) or (Amount), a construction such as "handsome desk" will only receive a reading representing it to mean a desk with beauty and dignity. There will be no representation of it as meaning one that is gracious or one that is moderately large, for these conceptually incongruous senses will be selected out. Limiting cases of this sort of selection will be those like "handsome sickness" that will receive no derived reading at all because the selection restrictions in the readings for the senses of "handsome" are not satisfied by the semantic markers in the reading for "sickness." Linguistic constructions of this type are semantically anomalous or meaningless, and this fact is represented by the absence of any reading associated with them.

Given selection restrictions, the projection rule will only produce derived readings that represent real senses of the constituents to which they are assigned. Assuming that the projection rule works from the bottom to the top of a phrase marker, from the syntactically minimal to the syntactically maximal constituents of a sentence, the derived readings assigned to its constituents reflect their compositional senses. The result of the operation of the projection rule will be a pairing of a set of readings with each node of the phrase marker, where the readings in the set represent the senses of the constituent dominated by the node.

Projection rules enforce selection restrictions. Where they are satisfied, projection rules combine readings to form derived readings that represent the senses of syntactically complex constituents. Since the projection rules form derived readings for syntactically complex constituents from the readings of their component constituents, the terminal elements of the underlying phrase marker must already have lexical readings associated with them before projection rules can be applied. This association is accomplished by the following convention:

(5.18)   The set of lexical readings R is associated with the terminal element D of the underlying phrase marker U just in case D was introduced into U by (4.25) from the lexicon entry $[D[C]]$ and R is paired with $[D[C]]$ in the dictionary.

When (5.18) has been applied in the case of each terminal element of an underlying phrase marker, the resulting *terminally interpreted underlying phrase marker* is subject to the application of the projection rule. The projection rule operations differ from one another in that each operation applies in the case of a different grammatical relation and effects different combinatorial steps to form a derived reading. Thus certain projection operations apply first to a terminally interpreted underlying phrase marker. When these have formed derived readings and associated them with the appropriate constituents in the underlying phrase marker, other operations become applicable and combine the derived readings to form other derived readings. When this interpretive process is completed, each constituent, including the whole sentence itself, will have been assigned a set of readings. An underlying phrase marker each of whose constituents is assigned a set of readings by such a process will be referred to as a *semantically interpreted underlying phrase marker*.

We considered the nature of semantic representation because we found that to formally reconstruct commonsense definitions of semantic properties and relations we need to refer to the formal features of these representations. Let us now present some examples of how commonsense definitions are replaced by ones stated in terms of formal features of semantic representations.

(5.19)   A constituent is semantically unique just in case it has exactly one reading in the set assigned to it.

(5.20)   A constituent is semantically ambiguous (n-ways) just in case the set of readings assigned to it has n members, $n > 1$.

(5.21)   A constituent C_i is (on one sense) synonymous with another C_j just in case the set of readings assigned to C_i and C_j have a member in common.

If a pair of constituents meeting this condition are sentences, then they are paraphrases (on a sense).

(5.22) A constituent C_i is fully synonymous with another C_j just in case the set of readings assigned to them is identical. If a pair of constituents meeting this condition are sentences, then they are full paraphrases.

(5.23) A constituent C_i is semantically distinct from another C_j just in case the sets of readings assigned to them have no common members.

(5.24) A constituent C_i is semantically similar to another C_j just in case the sets of readings assigned to them have a proper subset in common. C_i and C_j are thus semantically similar with respect to the concepts represented by the semantic markers in this proper subset.

(5.25) A constituent C_i is semantically included in another C_j (with respect to a sense of each) just in case every semantic marker in a reading of C_i also appears in a reading of C_j but that reading of C_j contains some semantic markers not in the given reading of C_i.

(5.26) A constituent is semantically anomalous just in case the set of readings assigned to it is empty.

(5.27) A constituent C is semantically redundant in the sentence S just in case the reading of C in the semantically interpreted underlying phrase marker of S has been formed from a reading of a modifier c_1 and a reading of its head c_2 and the reading of c_1 contains only semantic markers appearing in the reading of c_2.

The semantic interpretation of a particular underlying phrase marker is its semantically interpreted
underlying phrase marker together with all the statements that follow from this semantically interpreted
underlying phrase marker and the definitions of semantic properties and relations in semantic theory. The
semantic interpretation of a sentence S is the set of
semantically interpreted underlying phrase markers
associated with *S* together with the set of statements
about *S* that follow from them and the definitions of
semantic properties and relations in semantic theory.

These statements about the semantic properties and
relations of a sentence play a fundamental role in the
empirical confirmation of a semantic component of a
transformational grammar, for they comprise the predictions that the component makes about the data. Accordingly, the evidence for a semantic component
consists in statements that correctly predict which sentences speakers judge to be semantically anomalous,
which they judge to be semantically ambiguous, which
they judge to be synonymous, and so forth. If certain
statements in the semantic interpretation of a sentence
prove false, then the semantic component must be revised appropriately; and if there are semantic properties and relations that speakers attribute to a sentence
but that are not predicted by any of the statements in
its semantic interpretation, then the semantic component must be suitably extended. Hence the empirical
investigation of the semantics of a natural language is
no different in principle from that of other phenomena
in other sciences, for in semantics also, a hypothesis

about an underlying reality obtains its empirical justification from success in predicting and explaining publically accessible data on the basis of its hypothesis about the structure of the underlying reality.

Formal definitions of other semantic properties and relations asked about in (5.1)–(5.10) and of further semantic properties and relations depend on constructing more revealing forms of semantic representation. Indeed, progress in semantics depends on the mutual development of semantic representation and of definitions of semantic properties and relations. We cannot progress very far in defining semantic properties and relations without developing deeper and more revealing representations of meaning because such definitions must be framed in terms of the formal structure of such representations. But, also, we cannot obtain deeper and more revealing representations of meaning without further and more sophisticated definitions of semantic properties and relations. The reason is simple. The formal make-up of a semantic representation has to be justified on the grounds that it reflects semantic structure, and such justification can come only from the intuitions of native speakers about the semantic structure of the words, phrases, clauses, and sentences for which the semantic representation is given. Thus the evidence for a semantic representation must take the form of a claim that such intuitions support the hypothesis that the semantic representation assigned to a linguistic construction correctly represents its semantic structure. But semantic intuitions always take the form of judgments that the construction has one or another semantic property or relation. So in order to tell whether such intuitions do support an hypothesis, we must know what predictions the semantic representation makes about the semantic properties and relations of the construction to which it is assigned, and whether they agree with the speakers' judgments about them. Because definitions of semantic properties and relations tell us what predictions the semantic representation makes about the construction, they provide an essential step in empirical justification, without which progress toward deeper and more revealing semantic representations is impossible.

If the approach to the study of meaning outlined above is generally right, then our perspective on semantics must undergo as radical a change as our perspective on syntax has undergone as a consequence of the transformational conception of grammar. We have to stop trying to find something that meets *a priori* non-Democritean standards of objectivity. We should not look to base a theory of meaning on publically observable features of the environment, such as the things referred to in the use of language, the stimuli controlling verbal responses, or the conditions that determine the appropriate use of words, but instead look to base the theory on the same kind of underlying reality that our theory of deep structure in syntax is based on. This follows directly from the fact that the semantic interpretation of a sentence must be determined by aspects of its underlying phrase markers, that it cannot be determined by surface structure. To show that this is indeed so, we only have to observe that the semantic interpretation of a sentence has to provide an analysis of its meaning that exhibits its meaning as a compositional function of the meanings of its parts, and to observe further that the arguments considered in Chapter 4 show that there is an underlying syntactic reality are also arguments to show that the full syntactic information required for a compositional analysis, particularly the constituents of the sentence and their grammatical relations, is not available in surface structure.[49]

Casting semantics as a further aspect of the underlying reality of language does not mean that a theory of meaning will lack objectivity, as non-Democriteans fear. It need no more lack objectivity than did early Democritean theory or transformational syntactic theory. The objectivity of claims about meaning will derive from the public evidence from overt behavior of fluent speakers and the logical relations established between such evidence and the claims of semantic theory that it supports.

It was fear of linguistic theories that are devoid of objectivity that prompted taxonomic linguists like Bloomfield and his followers to hold that grammars should receive a physicalistic interpretation as systems of segmentation and classification of the physical

[49]Cf. J.J. Katz and P. Postal, *An Integrated Theory of Linguistic Descriptions*. There is a controversy at present about whether surface structure provides any information relevant to semantic interpretation, but its outcome in no way affects the point here. Those who wish to look at this controversy should consult N. Chomsky, "Deep Structure, Surface Structure, and Semantic Interpretation," in *Studies in General and Oriental Linguistics*, edited by R. Jakobson·and S. Kawamoto (Tokyo: TEC Corporation, 1970); and J. J. Katz, *Semantic Theory*, ch. 8, sec. 4.

sounds of actual speech. This narrow reductionism was intended to avoid the lack of objectivity that appeared to be a necessary concomitant of a mentalistic interpretation of grammars. Bloomfield once wrote:

> The testing of this hypothesis of *physicalism* will be the task of the next generations, and linguists will have to perform an important part of the work. Non-linguists . . . constantly forget that a speaker is making noise, and credit him, instead, with the possession of impalpable 'ideas', . . . the noise is sufficient. . . .[50]

We have shown that the taxonomic "library classification" model of grammars is inadequate because its basic assumption that the structure of sentences reduces ultimately to physical segments of utterances makes no place for the underlying reality of linguistic structure. This means that linguists can no longer interpret grammars in such external, physicalistic terms, but must think of them as explications of the linguistic competence of fluent speakers, i.e., as explications of their internalized knowledge of the rules that govern sound–meaning relations in their language. Furthermore, this implies that grammars must receive a mentalistic interpretation. For if the underlying reality of language determines the surface form of sentence structure and is itself identified with the competence of speakers, the principles of grammar that describe the underlying reality and its transformational relation to the shape of utterances must describe something that is mental or conceptual in some sense.

But, although we are committed to rejecting Bloom-

---

[50]L. Bloomfield, "Language or Ideas?," *Language*, vol. 12, (1936), 89–95.

fieldian physicalism and accepting some form of mentalism, what form of mentalism we accept is still left open. As I have pointed out elsewhere,[51] the form of mentalism that is appropriate to transformation theory has nothing whatever to do with the kind of mentalism that Bloomfield objected to. His horror of mentalistic concepts was based on the mistaken belief that to introduce mentalistic concepts of any sort into linguistics would immediately make linguistics forgo any claim to the status of an objective science. But this belief was the result of his assuming that mentalism in any form was a species of spiritualism or soul psychology that is inconsistent with a causal view of nature. There is no reason to take mentalism in this way. We can instead take it to be an interpretation of grammars on which they offer an hypothesis about the mechanism inside the heads of fluent speakers that contains the principles of sound-meaning correlation which are applied in the production and recognition of speech. The hypothesis itself need not be presented in terms of neurophysiology, though it may some day be put into this form.

---

[51]See J. J. Katz, "Mentalism in Linguistics," *Language*, vol. 40, No. 2 (April-June 1964), 124–37; reprinted together with a companion piece about the issues in the philosophy of science that are related to the question of mentalism in linguistics, called "On the Existence of Theoretical Entities," in *The Structure and Psychology of Language*, edited by T. Bever and W. Weksel (New York: Holt, in press). The conception of mentalism presented in these articles should be taken into consideration not only in evaluating claims like those of Bloomfield but in evaluating claims like Goodman's that meanings are "ghostly entities" that "lie between words and their extension." Cf. N. Goodman, "On Likeness of Meaning," *Semantics and the Philosophy of Language*, p. 70. Extensionalists like Goodman make their theories seem more attractive by making it appear that the only alternative is some sort of soft-headed spiritualism.

It is crucial to make explicit that we do not take the grammar that linguists write for a natural language to be the description of what actual speakers have in their heads. Rather, we take grammars to be idealizations of actual cases in much the same sense in which perfectly rigid rods, perfect vacuums, and frictionless planes are. Thus, a grammar can best be taken to be a theory of the competence of an *ideal* speaker whose knowledge of the language is perfect. This idealization from the imperfect knowledge of real speakers is, then, motivated by the same considerations that make it necessary to introduce ideal objects into physics and other sciences, namely, formulating the principles and laws of a science in terms of ideal objects and systems, instead of actual ones, enables theories in that science to disregard extraneous factors and thereby to provide simpler and more revealing accounts of the relations that determine the phenomena. Thus just as the idealization of a frictionless plane enables physical theory to disregard frictional differences in its formulation of laws of motion, so the idealization of a perfectly fluent speaker enables linguistic theory to disregard accidental performance differences, such as incomplete linguistic knowledge, memory limitations, etc., in its formulation of rules of grammar.

Construing grammars as idealizations of actual speakers enables us to adopt a mentalistic interpretation of grammars without identifying phonological objects such as phonemes or features, syntactic objects such as nouns, verbs, phrases, etc., or semantic objects such as senses or meanings with particular aspects of

the mental apparatus in the minds or brains of real
speakers or communities of them. This is particularly
important at the semantic level because of the general
tendency to suppose that senses or meanings are psychological objects, that they are ideas or thoughts or
kinds of ideas or thoughts. But just as we can distinguish
at the levels of phonology and syntax between an utterance and a sentence, so here we can distinguish between a thought or idea and a meaning. Ideas,
thoughts, cognitions, etc., like utterances, are performance phenomena, while meanings, like phonological
features and syntactic categories, are abstractions that
form part of competence. This point coincides, I think,
with Frege's reason for denying that *Gedanken* are to
be identified with anything psychological.[52] He observed that the *Gedanke* expressed in statements of the
Pythagorean theorem does not belong to any one person in the sense in which ideas, thoughts, feelings, sen-
sations, wishes, or anything else psychological does. The
idea, thought, feeling, etc., that one has belongs to one
(he is its bearer) and he is unique in this, for no two
people can have the same idea, thought, feeling, etc.
We speak of John's wish, my thought, your idea, but not
of John's Pythagorean theorem, my Pythagorean theorem, or your Pythagorean theorem in this sense of
possession. Second, Frege observed that the *Gedanke*
expressed in a statement of the Pythagorean theorem

[52]G. Frege, "The Thought: A Logical Inquiry," in *Essays on Frege*, E. D.
Klemke, ed. (Urbana: University of Illinois Press, 1968), pp. 507–536; also
reprinted in *Philosophical Logic*, edited by P. F. Strawson (Oxford: Oxford
University Press, 1967), pp. 26–38.

is timeless; it cannot be dated. But ideas, thoughts, feelings, etc., are temporally specifiable. We speak of the thought someone is now thinking, the wish he had on his birthday, or the feeling he will have when he receives the bad news, but not of the Pythagorean theorem of the present, of yesterday, etc. Third, Frege observes that the *Gedanke* expressed by a statement of the Pythagorean theorem does not come into existence in the first act of thinking it, as does my idea that I might have lost my wallet in the car or my memory that I did lose it in the car. Rather, as Frege says, when one first apprehends a *Gedanke* one comes to stand in a certain relation to something that already exists, as is implied by saying that one discovers theorems. Such considerations carry over to the distinction between meanings and thoughts, ideas, etc., quite easily if one understands all elements of linguistic competence as aspects of an idealization representing the perfect knowledge of an ideal speaker, as an abstraction from the actual knowledge of real speakers. The actual speakers' knowledge of the meaning of words and sentences is, then, an imperfect facsimile of their meaning in the language, which is given by an idealized grammar.

6.

On The Philosophical Import of Underlying Linguistic Reality

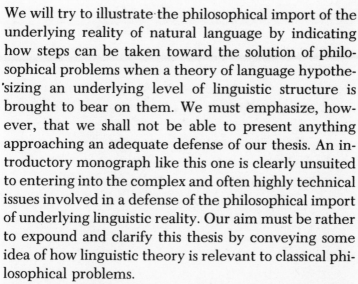

We will try to illustrate the philosophical import of the underlying reality of natural language by indicating how steps can be taken toward the solution of philosophical problems when a theory of language hypothesizing an underlying level of linguistic structure is brought to bear on them. We must emphasize, however, that we shall not be able to present anything approaching an adequate defense of our thesis. An introductory monograph like this one is clearly unsuited to entering into the complex and often highly technical issues involved in a defense of the philosophical import of underlying linguistic reality. Our aim must be rather to expound and clarify this thesis by conveying some idea of how linguistic theory is relevant to classical philosophical problems.

For this purpose, we have chosen three problems, each presenting a facet of the rationalist-empiricist controversy. The first problem is one of the two components of the traditional philosophical problem of perception. We shall refer to it as "the problem of percept determination." It can be formulated in the following question: How are knowledge, beliefs, expectations, etc., used to interpret sensory signals; what is the nature of the relation between a sensory signal and the resulting percept? To make these questions more concrete, we can think of the sensory signal in the usual way as physical stimulation of sensory receptors and we can think of a percept as a mental representation of what is perceived in cases of veridical perception and what remains invariant from such cases to cases of illusory or hallucinatory perception that are indistinguishable from them.

The other component of the problem of perception, which we shall call "the problem of knowledge determination," concerns how we justify claims to know something about the source of a sensory signal on the basis of information in the percept to which the signal has given rise. How a "dagger-percept" is formed in the mind of a Macbeth or of a person actually seeing a dagger is a question in the area of percept determination, while what are the conditions under which one is justified in claiming to see a dagger when having a dagger-percept is a question of knowledge determination. The full problem of perception is thus the question of how sensory stimulation can lead eventually to knowledge of the objects and events in the world.[53]

---

[53] The traditional answer is that such knowledge comes from the causal action of the physical environment on the sense organs, which produces neural impulses that travel along pathways from the sense organ to the brain, where the information carried by the impulses is processed, with the

We shall have nothing to say about this latter problem, but shall concentrate on the problem of percept determination. We can conveniently present this problem as the question of what kind of mechanism inside the "black box"

(6.1)   Physical signal ⟶ ▮ ⟶ Percept

specifies the relation between the inputs and outputs in perception.

There are two general theories about this kind of relation. There is the classical empiricist theory on which the organism is a passive receiver of sensory information. Perception, according to Hume, is "a mere passive admission of the impressions thro' the organs of sensation." And there is the rationalist theory on which the organism is an active constructor of percepts. Percepts, on the former theory, are internal recordings of sensory stimulation, and on the latter, ·objects that are formed from sensory information by a highly complex set of principles. The internal structure

mysterious result that perception occurs. If this processing in the brain has a different causal history, as in psychotic hallucinations and electrical stimulation of the brain, then percepts occur in the absence of an appropriate external physical stimulus, i.e., an experience etiologically different from but phenomenologically indistinguishable from perception occurs. Further, if the percept is the outcome of genuine perception but fails to portray the perceived object correctly, such as in cases where the impression of movement is conveyed by adjacent stationary lights which are illuminated in succession (the so-called "phi-phenomena"), the isolated phenomenological experience is again indistinguishable from cases of veridical perception. According to the traditional approach to the problem of knowledge determination, these three cases can be distinguished on the basis of general principles for comparing percepts with the perceiver's previous factual knowledge and for deciding in terms of such comparisons whether there is an external object and if so what its properties are.

of (6.1), according to empiricists, consists simply in a mechanism for forming an internal copy of the externally presented object based on the information in the impinging sensory stimulation. The mechanism inside the box is thus some sort of duplicating device or natural xerox machine. In contrast, according to the rationalist, the internal structure of (6.1) consists of a mechanism for internally generating percepts by a process in which much of their general organization and content is contributed by the perceiver himself.

To decide which of these general theories comes closest to the truth, we shall consider both as hypotheses about the internal structure found in (6.1), and ask which of them affords the best explanation of the input-output relation.

First, let us specialize the model (6.1) to the case of speech perception, so that we can bring what has been said about language in the previous sections to bear on this issue. The problem now takes the form of the question how does our linguistic knowledge, our grammatical competence, together with other types of knowledge, beliefs, expectations, etc., function in the process whereby speech perception arises from the input of an auditory signal under appropriate conditions.

The input of (6.1) is now considered an acoustic signal, a pattern of sound waves; and the percept the utterance which is heard at the termination of the causal process initiated by the mechanical effect of the signal on the inner ear. The input can be characterized in terms of the information contained in spectrographic records of speech sound. The output can be characterized in terms of the information contained in the linguistic description of the utterance that is provided by an optimal grammar of the language. Of course, not all the information in such descriptions is open to conscious awareness, but this does not matter for our purposes, since claims that the perceiver has such tacit knowledge as part of what he unconsciously perceives can be verified indirectly in experiments or on the basis of inferences from other introspective or behavioral facts.

Thus what the competing hypotheses about the internal structure of (6.1) must explain is how the percepts in speech perception come to have the phonological, syntactic, and semantic properties and relations marked in the linguistic descriptions of a transformational grammar. That is, they must explain how it is that acoustic signals come to be perceptually interpreted in terms of such properties and relations as grammaticality, alliteration, ambiguity, synonymy, analyticity, etc. This issue concerns the speaker's competence rather than his performance. It is thus a question about whether or not his perceptual ability presupposes antecedent knowledge concerning the structure of the class of possible percepts that must play a role in his perceptual interpretation of acoustic signals rather than a question about the actual strategies he utilizes to put such linguistic knowledge to use.

Looking at the issue in this way, we can see that the empiricist's copy theory is a false account of speech perception. For since the sensory inputs from which the speech-percepts are alleged to arise are characteris-

tically far less rich in information than the percepts
themselves, there cannot be anything even approaching the point-for-point correspondence between acoustic signals and percepts implied by the copy theory.
Thus it must fail to explain how percepts in speech
perception come to have their phonological, syntactic,
and semantic characteristics. Even with respect to the
phonological characteristics of percepts, it can be dem-
onstrated, by comparing spectrograms or other records
of acoustic signals with what is heard, that many of the
phonetic characteristics of the heard utterance have no
physical correlates and thus are not a function of the
acoustic signal. The hearer thus frequently makes use
of his knowledge of super-phonetic structure (i.e., syntactic and even semantic properties of the language) to
compensate for the missing correlates.[54]

In addition, it is abundantly clear from our earlier
discussion of the differences between the underlying
and surface structures of sentences that many of the
syntactic and semantic properties and relations of sentential percepts have no physical correlates in their
acoustic signals. Even if one grants the copy theory that
the acoustic signal contains the full surface structure of
a sentence, still, as shown in Chapter 4, it cannot account for the syntactic properties and relations in the
deep structure that are not reflected in the surface

[54]See P. Lieberman, *Intonation, Perception, and Language* (Cambridge:
M.I.T. Press, 1967), ch. 8, pp. 162–170; and the papers in the section "Speech
Perception," in *Psycholinguistics: A Book of Readings,* edited by S. Saporta
(New York: Holt, 1961), pp. 97–175.

structure. Since the semantic properties and relations of a sentence depend on just such underlying syntactic structure as is unexplainable on the supposition that it is copied from features of the physical signal, these properties and relations, too, are found not to be functions of the acoustic signal and so not to be accounted for on the copy theory.

Hence, it is necessary to hypothesize some set of mental mechanisms as part of the internal structure of the perceptual model whose operations are sufficient to relate informationally rich percepts to informationally impoverished acoustic signals. We have to assume that any information in a percept that is without a physical correlate in the acoustic signal that gives rise to the percept is provided by such mechanisms, instantiating aspects of the speaker's internalized knowledge of the grammar, since if such information does not come from the acoustic signal, it can only come from the speaker himself, supplied somehow in the process of identifying and understanding a signal, as his contribution to the formation of the percept which interprets the signal. If we were to adopt the copy theory, no explanation of the information in the percept that goes beyond that in the signal would be possible. So it is necessary to adopt some assumption that permits an explanation of the presence of such information in terms of the contribution of the speaker.

Since we can think of the acoustic signal in (6.1) as providing the information in the superficial phrase marker for a sentence, and the percept in (6.1) as providing the information in the semantically interpreted underlying phrase marker for the same sentence, the problem is to find an assumption which credits the speaker with knowledge of rules that determine a mapping of semantically interpreted underlying phrase markers onto superficial phrase markers for an infinite range of cases. The only assumption that qualifies is, therefore, that his contribution comes from his linguistic competence, his internalized knowledge of the grammar, since it is the grammar, and the grammar alone, that provides the proper mapping over the infinite range of sentences.

Is there any reason to think that the rationalist hypothesis, assuming it is required in the case of speech perception, is also required for other forms of perception? The existence of a wide range of cases in which there is an isomorphism between features of speech percepts and visual percepts suggests that the same type of explanation that succeeds in accounting for these properties and relations in speech perception may also account for them in visual perception. By way of following up this suggestion, I shall mention a variety of cases of this isomorphism. My intention is not to show that every property or relation in one area is isomorphic to one in the other but to show that the range of isomorphic properties and relations is far from trivial.

Corresponding to the distinction between grammatical and ungrammatical strings of words, there is the distinction in visual perception between distorted and undistorted images, and corresponding to degrees of ungrammaticality[55] there are degrees of visual distortion. Ungrammatical strings such as

(6.2)   run which bark therefore chiefly the a of when

correspond to certain kaleidoscopic images in which the parts of things are attached at the wrong places. Corresponding to syntactically ambiguous sentences such as

(6.3)   The shooting of the hunters was frightful

and other ambiguous cases like those cited in Section 4, there are the ambiguous figures found in texts on the psychology of perception. For example,

(6.4)

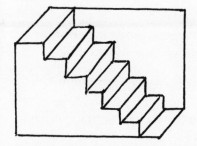 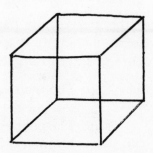

Corresponding to semantically anomalous sentences, there are surrealist paintings such as some of the more extraordinary paintings of Salvador Dali (as contrasted

---

[55]See the papers by Chomsky, Ziff, and Katz in the section "Extensions of Grammar," in *The Structure of Language: Readings in the Philosophy of Language*, pp. 384–416.

with straightforward representational paintings). Corresponding to contradictory sentences, there are impossible figures like

(6.5)

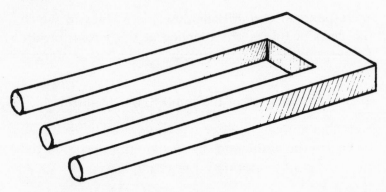

or the marvelously paradoxical drawings of Escher.[56] Corresponding to cases of synonymous expressions or sentences, for example, actives and passives like

(6.6) (i) The man who had his money stolen called the police

  (ii) The police were called by the man who had his money stolen

and other stylistic variants like (4.28) (i) and (ii), there are different views of the same object or scene. Corresponding to ellipsis, for example, (4.56), there is the phenomenon that Gestalt psychologists call "closure" in which an incompleted figure, for example,

[56]M.C. Escher, *Graphical Works* (London: Oldbourne Press, 1961).

(6.7)

is interpreted perceptually as though it were completed.[57] Corresponding to the way in which the same
constituent can mean different things in different sentential contexts, i.e., to the way sentential contexts can
alter the interpretation of a constituent—compare the
meaning of

(6.8)   the shooting of the men

with its meaning in the two sentences

(6.9)   The shooting of the men was inaccurate

(6.10)   The shooting of the men will be done by a firing
         squad

—there is the way in which the same line can appear
to be of different lengths in a pair of drawings like

[57]See K. Koffka, *Principles of Gestalt Psychology* (New York: Harcourt
Brace Jovanovich, 1935), pp. 167–168.

(6.11)

Corresponding to a sentence like

(6.12)   That the small girl hit the giant surprised us

which orthographically contains the sentence "The giant surprised us," even though this sentence is grammatically not one of its constituents, there are the "hidden pictures" that provide amusing puzzles for little children. Finally, corresponding to sentences like (4.35) and (4.36), there are cases in visual perception like those of the Ames Demonstrations based on the principle of equivalent retinal configurations, e.g., the case of the wire chair or the distorted room.[58]

These examples of isomorphism do not, of course, provide a conclusive argument for the rationalist hypothesis in the case of visual perception, nor are they intended as such. The argument presented in this section should be taken together with those offered by Gestalt psychologists as, rather, providing a basis for trying to develop an account of visual perception along rationalist lines. In the final analysis, only the success of such an account can provide a conclusive argument for

[58]W. H. Ittelson, *The Ames Demonstrations in Perception: A Guide to Their Construction and Use* (Princeton: Princeton University Press, 1952); W. H. Ittelson, *Visual Space Perception* (New York: Springer, 1961). Also F. P. Kilpatrick, ed., *Explorations in Transactional Psychology* (New York: New York University Press, 1961).

the rationalist hypothesis. Whether other kinds of perception can be shown to be isomorphic and so brought under the rationalist hypothesis depends on whether olfactory, tactile, etc., percepts have the appropriate structure.

Our next example of the philosophical import of the underlying reality of language concerns the nature of learning in the case of language acquisition. As in the discussion of perception, we can pose the question in terms of a model of the human capacity that makes the feat possible. In language acquisition, the model represents the innate capacity which a child employs to obtain an internalization of the grammar of the language of his community on the basis of the utterances and other relevant data he is exposed to in his early years. The model can be schematized:

(6.13)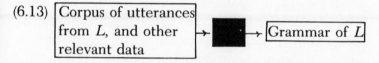

The question of how a language is learned thus becomes the question of what the internal structure of (6.13) must be to account for the fact that, without formal tutoring, children attain fluency just on the basis of a sample of the speech of their community and can achieve this within a very few years' time.

Here, too, we find an empiricist's theory and a rationalist's theory. The empiricist's maxim is *Nihil est in intellectu quod non prius fuerit in sensu* and his theory of learning, accordingly, assumes that innately the mind is a *tabula rasa,* equipped only with combinatorial devices for analyzing sensory data and for forming inductive generalizations from them. Thus Locke wrote:

> The senses at first let in *particular* ideas, and furnish the yet empty cabinet, and the mind by degrees growing familiar with some of them, they are lodged in the memory, and name got to them. Afterwards, the mind proceeding further, abstracts them, and by degrees learns the use of general names. In this manner the mind comes to be furnished with ideas and language, the *materials* about which to exercise its discursive faculty.[59]

Of course empiricists grant that certain ideas in the mind lack any direct counterpart in sense experience, but they hold that such ideas are formed from ideas given in sense experience either by composition, as when the idea of a golden mountain is formed from the separate ideas of gold and a mountain; by addition or subtraction from ideas given in sense experience, as when the idea of a giant or midget is formed from that of a normal sized man; or by analogy, as when the idea of a city one has never seen is formed from a city one has seen. The empiricist's doctrine is, then, that there are no ideas in the mature mind whose basic components were not originally delivered through the senses.

The rationalist, on the other hand, credits the innate structure of the mind with a rich system of abstract ideas that determines the general form of any knowledge it may acquire, since he finds it impossible to

[59]J. Locke, *An Essay Concerning Human Understanding* (Oxford: Oxford University Press, 1924), p. 22.

explain the acquisition of knowledge on the empiricist's doctrine. Thus Descartes wrote:

> . . . any man who rightly observes the limitations of the senses, and what precisely it is that can penetrate through this medium to our faculty of thinking must needs admit that no ideas of things, in the shape in which we envisage them by thought, are presented to us by the senses. So much so that in our ideas there is nothing which was not innate in the mind. . . . For nothing reaches our mind from external objects through the organs of sense beyond certain corporeal movements . . . but even these movements, and the figures which arise from them, are not conceived by us in the shape they assume in the organs of sense. . . . Could anything be imagined more preposterous than that all common notions which are inherent in our mind should arise from these movements, and should be incapable of existing without them?[60]

And Leibniz writes:

> The senses, although they are necessary for all our actual acquiring of knowledge, are by no means sufficient to give us the whole of our knowledge, since the senses never give anything but instances, particular or individual truths. Now all the instances which confirm a general truth, however numerous they may be, are not sufficient to establish the universal necessity of this same truth; for it does not follow that what has happened will happen in the same way. . . . The concatenations of ideas made by the lower animals are simply like those of mere empirics, who maintain that what has

[60]R. Descartes, "Notes Directed against a Certain Program," in *Philosophical Works of Descartes*, E. S. Haldane and G. R. T. Ross, trans. and ed. (New York: Dover, 1955) vol. II, pp. 442–443.

sometimes happened will happen again in a case which resembles the former in characteristics which strike them, although they are incapable of judging whether or not the same reasons hold good in both cases. That is why it is so simple a matter for men to entrap animals, and so easy for mere empirics to make mistakes.[61]

Thus the empiricist sees knowledge as built up, through an ascending process, out of sense impressions that get combined inductively by associative connections, whereas the rationalist sees it as formed, through a descending process, by the organization of sense experience in terms of innate ideas about the form of knowledge.

The particular form which the empiricist theory of learning takes in the case of language acquisition is that of a *discovery procedure* for grammars. As will be recalled from the discussion at the beginning of Chapter 4, a discovery procedure is a set of instructions for analyzing a corpus of utterances from a language and inductively extrapolating the optimal grammar. Although the original interest of taxonomic linguists in the construction of a discovery procedure was merely to equip the field linguist with formal procedures which can be applied mechanically and which automatically yield the optimal grammar when correctly applied to an adequate corpus,[62] the character of a discovery

[61]G. W. Leibniz, "New Essays on the Human Understanding," in *The Monadology and Other Philosophical Writings*, R. Latta, trans. (Oxford: Oxford University Press, 1898), p. 364.

[62]In C. F. Hockett, "A Formal Statement of Morphemic Analysis," in *Studies in Linguistics*, Vol. X (1952), 27, he says that his aim is to construct "formal procedures by which one can work from scratch to a complete description of the pattern of language."

procedure, as a device for constructing a grammar for a language with an antecedent guarantee of success, also makes it an hypothesis about the internal structure of (6.13). The child who has not yet learned a language and the field linguist who has no previous acquaintance with it are in very much the same position. Placed in an English-speaking community, they will have to acquire a grammar of English; in a Russian-speaking community, they will, with comparable facility, have to acquire a grammar of Russian; and so forth. The main difference, which is irrelevant to the dual role that a discovery procedure plays, is that what the child does is done on the basis of innate, covert capacities, while what the field linguist does is done, primarily, on the basis of learned, overt knowledge and skills developed in the course of his training. But from the empiricist viewpoint, both the child's capacities and the linguist's knowledge and skills can be best regarded as possession of a discovery procedure.

The particular form that the rationalist theory of learning takes in the case of language acquisition is that of an *evaluation procedure, viz.*, a criterion for making an empirically justified choice among a set of equally simple grammars, each compatible with the available evidence and each in the form prescribed by linguistic theory.[63] Like a discovery procedure, an evaluation procedure can serve either as a methodological apparatus for the field linguist or as an hypothesis about

[63]See the discussion in Chapter 3 of this monograph and N. Chomsky, *Syntactic Structures*, ch. 6.

the internal structure of (6.13). In the latter capacity, the procedure constitutes a nativist theory of how the child learns. The child must make essentially the same choices as the linguist; each chooses a new grammar or reaffirms his previous choice whenever his corpus of available data increases. On the rationalist theory, the child chooses an optimal grammar from among a set of possible grammars determined by innate principles about the form of human language, the choice itself being governed by the requirement that the grammar selected be the simplest among the possible grammars that best predict the data available at the point of choice.[64]

The rationalist-transformationalist theory takes the child's innate ideas about language to be the content of the universals in the (transformational) theory of grammar. That is, the child, though he cannot be assumed to know what particular language he is going to learn, can know, tacitly, that it is one of a quite restricted set of possible languages meeting the constraints imposed by these universals. Thus he is assumed to know, innately, that the grammar of the language has the form of a transformational grammar as given in phonological, syntactic, and semantic theory, i.e., the form of the rules in each component, the constructs out of which actual rules can be formulated, and the principles for organizing such rules into a system. Given this knowledge, the child can *a priori* construct the class of possible grammars, independently of any empirical data.

[64]See *Aspects of the Theory of Syntax*, ch. 1, sec. 7.

The evaluation procedure enables him to order these grammars on the basis of their complexity. Then, making use of the corpus of utterances he is exposed to, he can test the grammars that rank simplest on this ordering by employing the structure assignment algorithm to deduce from the grammars predictions about the phonological, syntactic, and semantic properties of the utterances in the corpus. The grammar he eventually adopts is therefore the simplest one compatible with the total sum of his linguistic experience.[65] Accordingly, the rationalist-transformational theory conceives of language learning as a process of verification and refutation of theories, much like the sort of process that goes on in the more advanced natural sciences; but the empiricist-taxonomic theory conceives of it as the sort of inductive generalization from data that goes on in statistical investigations.

To sum up, the taxonomic theory represents the empiricist viewpoint on the question of language acquisition, and the transformational theory represents the rationalist. The former theory holds that procedures of segmentation and classification together with inductive generalization—or what amounts to the same thing, principles of associative learning—can account for mastery of a language without assuming any innate content in the mind beyond such data-processing procedures and inductive generalization. The latter holds that un-

[65]What is said here presents a conception of the nature of language learning, but, of course, not an actual theory of the performance side of the process. See N. Chomsky, *Aspects of the Theory of Syntax*, ch. 1, p. 202, footnote 19 and J.J. Katz, *The Philosophy of Language*, pp. 240–282.

less the general form of the mature speaker's competence (the universals of language in the theory of grammar) is also assumed to be innate, it is not possible to
account for the speaker's mastery of his language.

When the empiricist and rationalist viewpoints are
made precise, as hypotheses about the nature of language learning, one can bring to bear considerable evidence from linguistics to support the rationalist
viewpoint. This evidence can be thought of as developing and strengthening the Cartesian-Leibnizian argument, cited above, that the information provided by
the senses so much underdetermines the character of
the mature knowledge that the totality of such knowledge cannot possibly come from sensory information
alone.

Even under the charitable assumption that the discovery procedure works perfectly, the empiricist-taxonomic theory of language acquisition fails because the
grammar obtained from any finite sample of utterances
by the mechanisms of segmentation, classification, and
inductive generalization will not be a descriptively adequate grammar. This is because such procedures necessarily yield taxonomic grammars, and since, as shown in
Chapter 4, no taxonomic grammar can be an empirically adequate grammar of a natural language, it follows that no discovery procedure can account for the
acquisition of the sort of grammar that actually underlies fluency in a natural language.

Some linguists have claimed that a discovery procedure is logically neutral toward competitive theories
about the nature of language. But no reasonable inter-

pretation of the notion 'discovery procedure' can pre-
serve such neutrality since adopting a discovery procedure makes at least two assumptions about the nature
of language: first, that every language has all and only
elements which satisfy the distributional definitions of
the procedure; second, that the rules of the grammar
can be stated in terms of just these distributionally discovered elements and that the rules at any given level
of an analysis (phonemic, morphemic, word, phrase,
etc.) can make no use of information from rules at any
higher level.[66] If the first fails, then either there will be
some elements of the language which the procedure
will fail to isolate or else the procedure will isolate some
elements not possessed by the language; if the second
fails, there will be some rules of the language which
cannot be stated in terms of the discovered elements
and permissible relations. In either case the dis-

---

[66]It is perfectly clear that if such procedures are to work in a step-by-step
mechanical fashion, then no appeal to higher-level elements can be made
in the determination of lower-level ones. Thus the segmentation and classification at any particular level can only appeal to distributional facts from
lower levels or from already determined cases at that level. For example, at
the phonological level, the distributional facts which a discovery procedure
can bring to bear cannot include the fact that a certain sequence of phonological elements always occurs in such and such a position with respect to
a certain morpheme class, since morpheme classes must be discovered after
all the phoneme classes have been discovered. Similarly, no information
about syntactic constituents or word boundaries can be used to help in
determining the definitions of morphemic elements, since such information
is logically consequent to morphological determination. When these requirements of order are not met, taxonomic linguists will invariably level the
charge of circularity against the "offending" description. These are not
arbitrary criticisms; rather, they stem directly from the taxonomic assumption that grammars are to be constructed from a corpus on the basis of
distributional facts revealed by techniques of substitution in diagnostic environments, where the environments themselves must be specified by the
same substitution techniques or the results thereof.

covery procedure would have to be deemed inadequate, since the assumption of its adequacy depends on the truth of both these assumptions about language. They are presuppositions for successful application of the instructions in the procedure, just as the normal assumptions we make about the physical properties of wood, nails, screws, and brackets, assumptions that glue sticks, that saws cut, etc., are presuppositions for successful application of instructions for making furniture out of materials such as wood, nails, etc., with tools such as saws, hammers, screwdrivers, etc. Consequently, claims about the neutrality of discovery procedures are false. Discovery procedures not only make extremely strong claims about the nature of language, but worse yet, these claims are themselves false.

However, our primary concern is to support the Cartesian-Leibnizian argument against empiricism by explaining why the grammar that constitutes what a speaker learns in acquiring a language cannot, in principle, be discovered by such procedures. Let us then suppose, for the sake of argument, that the input to (6.13) provides all the information contained in the surface phrase markers for the sentences in the corpus to which the language learner has been exposed during his formative period. We can assume further that the grammar acquired on the basis of this information is a transformational grammar of the sort described in Chapters 4 and 5, which is to say that what must be accounted for are rules that connect surface phrase markers with sets of underlying phrase markers, i.e., transformations. Accordingly, it must be the case that a discovery procedure can obtain the information in underlying phrase markers from that in their corresponding surface phrase marker by procedures of segmentation, classification, and inductive generalization applied to the surface phrase marker. This implies that the relation in which the constituent structure represented in surface phrase markers stands to the constituent structure represented in their underlying phrase markers is that in which an inductive regularity found in a sample of observed cases stands to the regularity in the population that can be inductively generalized from it. Since inductive generalizations are inferences wherein some property observed to hold for the members of the sample is projected to hold also for the rest of the population from which the sample was drawn, the regularity in the population must be exactly the one observed in the sample. This means that for the empiricist theory to be true either there are only surface phrase markers for sentences, as in taxonmic grammars, or else underlying phrase markers can contain no structure or property that is not found in the surface phrase marker correlative to them. This, however, is flatly contradicted by the entire body of evidence (cf. Chapter 4) which established the theory of transformational grammar. For this evidence clearly shows that the relation between the constituent structure represented in surface phrase markers to the constituent structure represented in underlying phrase markers does not even approximate an inductive relation. Being transformational, the relation is the opposite of inductive; it is a relation between structurally impoverished surface structure and richly complex deep structure. Inductive extrapolation thus cannot explain the acquisition of grammatical rules that represent deep structure and its relation to surface structure or the semantic properties and relations that are determined by deep structure.[67]

The last of the philosophical problems to be taken up in this brief attempt to indicate how the results of linguistic theory illustrate the philosophical import of the underlying reality of language is the question of whether there are necessary truths. We shall concern ourselves with one form that this question takes in recent philosophy of language, namely, the issue of the existence of a sharp analytic-synthetic distinction.

The attack launched in the fifties and sixties against

[67]The reader who wishes to go beyond the sketch of the argument against the empiricist theory presented in the text is referred to the following works. N. Chomsky, "Explanatory Models in Linguistics," in *Logic, Methodology, and Philosophy of Science*, E. Nagel, P. Suppes, and A. Tarski, eds. (Stanford: Stanford University Press, 1962), pp. 528–550; *Cartesian Linguistics; Recent Contributions to the Theory of Innate Ideas*," *Synthese*, vol. 17, No. 1, (March 1967), 2–11; *Language and Mind* (New York: Harcourt Brace Jovanovich, 1968), ch. 3. Also J.J. Katz, *The Philosophy of Language* (New York: Harper & Row, 1966), pp. 240–282. For criticism by two leading empiricists cf. N. Goodman, "The Epistemological Argument," *Synthese*, vol. 17, No. 1, (March 1967), 23–28; and H. Putnam, "The Innateness Hypothesis and Explanatory Models in Linguistics," *Synthese*, vol. 17, No. 1, (March 1967), 12–22. There are replies by Chomsky in *Language and Mind* and there are replies and rebuttals to replies, etc., in *Language and Philosophy*, S. Hook, ed. (New York: New York University Press, 1969), Part II.

the attempt, particularly by logical empiricists, to draw an analytic–synthetic distinction was not pressed by nonpartisan critics, disinterestedly seeking to expose a spurious distinction and the false conception of knowledge based on it. Nor was the attack mounted by partisan rationalists bent on formulating a rejoinder to the newest threat to their position, logical empiricism. Rather, the principal figures, Quine, Goodman, and White,[68] were themselves empiricists. Theirs was a criticism of an empiricist doctrine, by empiricists, and for the sake of empiricism. It was an internal conflict within the ranks of empiricism between a European school, logical empiricism, that had compromised with rationalist doctrines concerning necessary truth in adopting the idea of linguistic truth and a more extreme American wing that was unwilling to make this compromise. Therefore, this attack constituted a new and far more thoroughgoing empiricist challenge to the rationalist conception of necessity.

Quine's famous paper "Two Dogmas cf Empiricism" was the spearhead of this empiricist challenge.[69] He set out to show that even so attenuated a version of the doctrine of necessary truth as that found in the syntactical and semantical systems of Carnap and his followers were too much of a concession to rationalism. The trou-

---

[68]W. V. Quine, "Two Dogmas of Empiricism," in *From a Logical Point of View* (Cambridge: Harvard University Press, 1953), pp. 20–46; N. Goodman, "On Likeness of Meaning"; and M. White, "The Analytic and the Synthetic: An Untenable Dualism," in *Semantics and the Philosophy of Language* Urbana: Urbana University of Illinois Press, 1952), pp. 272–286.

[69]I deal only with Quine because his arguments are the most influential.

ble with Quine's argument, however, is that, although
it is only sufficient to purge the empiricist camp of the
Carnapian *rapprochement* with rationalism, it is not
valid as a criticism of every attempt to ground the doctrine of necessary truth on a distinction between the
analytic and the synthetic.[70]

Let us now attempt to explicate the Kantian conception of analyticity within the framework of the transformational theory of grammar.[71] For, as part of this
theory, it can be shown to be immune from Quinian
criticisms for certain quite specific reasons. Kant distinguished the class of analytic propositions by defining
them as those that express "nothing in the predicate
but what has been already thought in the concept of the
subject."[72] Accordingly, analytic propositions like those
expressed by the sentences

(6.14)   Southpaws are lefthanded
(6.15)   Nightmares are dreams
(6.16)   Bachelors are male

[70]Quine seems to have thought that his arguments in "Two Dogmas
of Empiricism" were relevant to any attempt to make the distinction.
He wrote: "But, for all its a priori reasonableness a boundary between analytic and synthetic statements simply has not been drawn. That there
is such a distinction to be drawn at all is an unempirical dogma of empiricists, a metaphysical article of faith." *From a Logical Point of View,* p.
37.

[71]J.J. Katz, "Analyticity and Contradiction in Natural Language," in *The
Structure of Language: Readings in the Philosophy of Language,* pp. 519–
543, and J.J. Katz, *The Philosophy of Language,* pp. 479–518. This theory
is revised in *Semantic Theory,* ch. 4.

[72]I. Kant, *The Critique of Pure Reason,* N. K. Smith trans. (New York:
Humanities Press, 1950), pp. 48–51.

do not enlarge, in the least, one's concept of southpaws, nightmares, or bachelors, but only analyze them, showing their conceptual components. Synthetic propositions, such as those expressed by the sentences

(6.17)   Southpaws are better at throwing curve balls
(6.18)   Nightmares are events occurring in deep sleep
(6.19)   Bachelors are less likely to marry as they grow older

do enlarge one's concept of the things to which their subject refers: (6.17) expands on the concept of left-handed pitchers by adding the further information that they are better at throwing curves.

This distinction has been subject to three different forms of criticism. First, it has been claimed that Kant's account is limited to subject–predicate statements and thus is too restrictive. Second, it has been claimed that the distinction rests on an unexplicated and highly metaphorical relation of containment, and hence, on *Gedanken* experiments to determine what is thought in thinking through a concept. Third, it has been claimed that it is not at all clear how we can empirically determine whether a sentence is analytic. The desire to answer these criticisms was my original motive for seeking a linguistic explication of the Kantian concept of analyticity.

The first criticism, that not all simple sentences are of subject–predicate form, has already been answered in the earlier part of this discussion. There we argued that grammar must distinguish two pairs of relational notions, the pair 'surface subject' and 'surface predicate', defined on final derived phrase markers, and the pair 'deep subject' and 'deep predicate', defined on underlying phrase markers. If we now give definitions of 'logical form' and 'grammatical form' that take advantage of these definitions of deep subject and predicate and surface subject and predicate, we can state the explication of the Kantian concept of analyticity so that it avoids objections that it applies to too restricted a set of sentences. That is:

(6.20)   The logical form of a sentence S in a language L_i is given by the set of semantically interpreted underlying phrase markers assigned to S by an optimal grammar of L_i together with the statements about the semantic properties and relations of S that follow from this set and the definitions of semantic properties and relations in semantic theory.

In short, the logical form of a sentence is given by its semantic interpretation. On the other hand:

(6.21)   The grammatical form of a sentence S in a language L_i is given by the phonetically interpreted superficial phrase marker assigned to S by an optimal grammar of L_i.[73]

[73]These two definitions implicitly draw a distinction between the representation of the logical form or grammatical form of a particular sentence from a natural language and the logical form and grammatical form for natural language in general. (6.20) says that the syntatic and semantic components of a transformational grammar of L_i provide a representation of the logical form of each sentence S in L_i in the form of semantically interpreted

Note also that the subject–predicate distinction used in the explication of analyticity is not the same as the copulative–noncopulative distinction, with which it is sometimes confused. Thus, sentences like

(6.22) [[kleptomaniacs]$_{\text{NP}}$ [are persons who steal out of a persistent neurotic impulse and without the motive of economic gain]$_{\text{VP}}$]$_{\text{S}}$

(6.23) [[kleptomaniacs]$_{\text{NP}}$ [steal out of a persistent neurotic impulse and without the motive of economic gain]$_{\text{VP}}$]$_{\text{S}}$

can both be handled by a straightforward explication of the Kantian concept of analyticity.

The second criticism can be answered by stating the Kantian concept within the formal vocabulary of semantic theory, i.e.,

(6.24) S is analytic $=_{\text{df}}$ the reading of the deep subject of S is a set of semantic markers that in-

underlying phrase markers that these components assign to S. (6.21) says that the syntactic and phonological components of a transformational grammar of L_i provide a representation of the grammatical form of each sentence S in L_i within the phonetically interpreted surface phrase marker that these components assign to S. But (6.20) also says that the properties and relations that distinguish the logical form of one sentence from that of another are explicated in the definitions stated in semantic theory. Thus, semantic theory constitutes a theory of logical form whose application is based on the representations that a transformational grammar gives of the sense of sentences. Semantic theory is a general theory of logical form, and particular grammars distinguish between the logical and grammatical form of individual sentences. Cf. J. J. Katz, "The Relevance of Linguistics to Philosophy," *The Journal of Philosophy*, Vol. LXII, No. 20 (October 1965), 590–602, and more recently, J.J. Katz, "Logic and Language: An Examination of Recent Criticisms of Intentionalism," (to appear).

cludes every semantic marker appearing in the reading for the deep predicate of S.

The apparatus of semantic representation in linguistic theory, particularly the use of semantic markers to formally represent the conceptual components of senses, and the relation of set inclusion, can replace the metaphorical or loose notions used by Kant of 'a concept', of 'thinking through a concept', and of 'concept containment'. Thus *Gedanken* experiments can be replaced by mechanically definable operations on formal representations of syntactic structure and sense.

The third criticism of Kant's account can be overcome by showing how empirical evidence can be brought to bear on the question of whether or not a sentence is analytic. To show this, we will provide a sketch of the manner in which predictions about the analyticity of sentences are obtained in linguistic theory and the way these predictions can be confirmed or disconfirmed on the basis of linguistic evidence.

Consider the sentence (6.16). We obtain a prediction of its analyticity if the semantic component of the grammar of English assigns (6.16) a semantically interpreted underlying phrase marker in which the deep subject receives the reading (6.25)

(6.25) (Physical Object) (Human) (Male) (Not Married) (Adult)

and the deep predicate receives the reading (6.26).

(6.26) (Male)

For if this is the case, the definition (6.24) of semantic theory will mark the sentence as analytic. We can verify the correctness of this prediction directly by asking native speakers if the sentence (6.16) is a case of redundant predication[74] or indirectly by appealing to their linguistic intuitions about other semantic properties and relations to justify (6.25) and (6.26). In the latter case, the linguistic intuitions of native speakers (as the English-speaking reader can verify for himself) enable us to state the following facts about the components of the meaning of "bachelor":

(6.27) One component of the meaning of "bachelor" is the concept of adulthood. This is shown by the fact that "bachelor" has a "degree holder" sense by not involving the concept of adulthood, e.g., "The intellectually precocious child became a bachelor at the age of seven" is not contradictory.

(6.28) One component of the meaning of "bachelor" is the concept of being unmarried. This is shown by the fact that "unmarried bachelor" is redundant.

(6.29) One component of the meaning of "bachelor" is the concept of being male. This is shown by the fact that "bachelor" contrasts with "spinster" in the way that the semantically similar words "boy," "brother," "uncle," "bull," "fa-

[74]We will discuss the direct verification of semantic predictions and objections to it below.

ther," etc., contrast with the semantically similar words "girl," "sister," "aunt," "cow,"
"mother," etc.

(6.30) One component of the meaning of "bachelor"
is the concept of being human. This is shown by
the fact that "There are bachelors" entails
"There are humans."

(6.31) One component of the meaning of "bachelor"
is the concept of a physical object. This is shown
by the fact that "The bachelor fell from the
53rd floor and broke both himself and the pavement when he landed" is meaningful but "The
shadow fell from the 53rd floor and broke both
itself and the pavement when it landed" is
semantically deviant.

Given such facts, we can justify (6.25) and, in turn, the
predictions that (6.16), (6.32), (6.33), and others are analytic

(6.32) Bachelors are unmarried
(6.33) Bachelors are human beings

while (6.34) and others are non-analytic.

(6.34) Bachelors are monarchs

Thus, empirical evidence can confirm or disconfirm
such predictions and can thereby check the correctness
of the hypotheses about lexical meaning from which
the predictions derive.

The above presentation was my original attempt to
provide a linguistic explication of the concept of

analyticity. Subsequently, the definition (6.24) proved too narrow, not marking some genuine cases of analytic sentences. It will be worthwhile to indicate, even if as briefly as is necessary here, what the difficulty is and how it can be overcome.[75] There are three reasons. First, there is the desire to state the best formulation of the definition available. Second, the revised definition provides further answer to the criticism that the Kantian notion of analyticity applies only to sentences of subject-predicate form. Third, an examination of this difficulty illustrates how the definition of analyticity and the definitions of semantic properties and relations generally are open to empirical confirmation and disconfirmation, just as are the readings to which they apply. Thus, it is clear that the basis from which predictions about such properties and relations are made, and also each of its components, are empirically determined both in being open to empirical test and in having disconfirmatory evidence as guide to revision.

To see the difficulty, we first observe that sentences like the following

(6.35)   Someone sells things to those who buy them from him
(6.36)   Someone kills whomever he murders

are indistinguishable from analytic sentences *except* in that, for these cases (on the senses where their pronouns are coreferential anaphorically), the meaning-inclusion relation holds between the sense of one

[75]For a more detailed discussion see J. J. Katz, *Semantic Theory*, ch. 4.

object, the direct object in sentence (6.36) and the indirect object in (6.35), and the senses of the verb, the
subject, and any other objects. Here the latter includes
the former, whereas in cases like (6.16), (6.32), (6.33),
and Kant's examples the sense of the subject includes
the sense of the full predicate. Is there any reason to
take this as an inessential feature in the explication
of analyticity and to account for cases like (6.35) and
(6.36) as analytic sentences under a single abstract definition?

A reason can be given along the following lines. We
noted in connection with a criticism of our theory that
it is incorrect, in general, to say that an analytic sentence is true.[76] For example, the sentence (6.37) is analytic,

(6.37)   The bachelor who was the first man to set foot
on the moon is male.

but it is not true, assuming an analysis of truth conditions of sentences in which the truth conditions are
defined in terms of a presupposition. That is, construing
the sentence to *presuppose* that a bachelor was the
individual who stepped on the moon before any other
man and to *assert* of this bachelor that he is male, we
find, empirically, that the presupposition is false, so that
there is nothing of which the assertion can be true or
false. Accordingly, the sentence cannot be true. The
point here is that 'being analytic' is a property of the

---

[76] J. J. Katz, "Unpalatable Recipes for Buttering Parsnips," *The Journal of
Philosophy*, vol. LXV, No. 2 (January 25, 1968), 38–40.

logical or semantic structure of the sentence while 'being true' is a relation between the sentence and the
world. Hence, the best we can say on the basis of linguistic considerations alone is that analytic sentences
express propositions whose form secures them against
falsehood. That is, if their presupposition is satisfied, so
that the entities referred to by both the conditions for
the sentence's truth and the conditions for the sentence's falsehood exist, then, if the sentence is analytic,
it has to be true; if the presupposition is not satisfied,
then the sentence can have no truth-value and hence
cannot be false.

Why should sentences having the logical or semantic
structure of analytic propositions be secured against
falsehood in this manner? The answer from a Kantian
perspective or on the basis of (6.24) runs as follows: If
a sentence is analytic in the Kantian sense, its truth
conditions require the objects satisfying its presupposition to have a property or properties which such objects
are already determined to possess, since insofar as the
meaning of the subject picks them out on the basis of
their having the property or properties required by the
truth conditions. Since a sentence is true in case its
subject succeeds in referring and what it refers to has
the property or properties that the truth conditions
require, then if the subject of an analytic sentence does
succeed in referring, what it refers to must have the
property or properties to satisfy the truth conditions.

From this, it can be concluded that the most general
feature of analytic sentences responsible for their
security against falsehood is that their truth conditions,

or assertion, are included in their presupposition, so that the former's being satisfied is by itself sufficient for the latter's being satisfied.

But, if this is so, sentences like (6.35) and (6.36) are also analytic, since their presupposition includes their truth condition. Consider a sentence like (6.38):

(6.38)   The president of the country shook hands with the bachelor who was the first man to step on the moon.

Like (6.37), this sentence is not true (and not false) because there is nothing in the world to which its truth conditions (or falsehood conditions) can apply. The truth conditions (and the falsehood conditions) of (6.38) apply to a pair of objects, one of which is the referent of its subject and the other the referent of its object. But no such pair of objects exists. If this construal of (6.38) is accepted, we have to say that objects as well as subjects can contribute to the presupposition of a sentence, and if we concede that there is no asymmetry between subject and object in this regard, we must also admit that our original definition of analyticity was wrong. Its error was to define analyticity too narrowly by identifying the source of analyticity in a sense-inclusion relation between the subject and predicate of a sentence.[77] A new definition is required that defines analyticity in terms of a relation of sense-inclusion whose range is not restricted to subjects but encompasses objects and any other constituent whose sense contributes to the pre-

[77]Cf. the discussion in J. J. Katz, *Semantic Theory,* ch. 4, sec. 5. I'm indebted to Paul Postal for first questioning this asymmetry claim.

supposition. A definition of this sort has been worked out,[78] but no more than the basic idea can be given here.

The idea is this: The reading of the sense of a simple declarative sentence represents its truth conditions as an n-placed predicate R and the components of its presupposition as a sequence of terms serving as the arguments of R. These terms are represented by readings of the Noun Phrases that function as the sentence's subject, direct object, indirect object, and so forth, and part of the formalism of the reading of the sentence correlates these readings of Noun Phrases with their proper places in the semantic representation of R. The new definition of analyticity says that a sentence is analytic just in case the reading of one of the terms of R, one component of the presupposition, contains the parts of the reading of the sentence that represents R and its other terms.

We now turn to an examination of Quine's claim to once and for all have refuted the rationalist attempt to establish *a priori* truths in the form of analytic statements. The feature of Quine's argument that prevents it from applying to any approach toward drawing the analytic-synthetic distinction is that it assumes that the explication of 'analytic' must be given on the basis of one of the three types of definition he considers, namely, *lexical definition*, which provides an expression synonymous with the definiendum; *explication*, wherein the definiens preserves aspects of the meaning of the definiendum but improves upon it in some way

[78] *Ibid.*

related to the special purpose of the explication; and *notational definition,* which introduces a new piece of notation and is nothing more than a convention for purposes of abbreviation.[79] But the type of definition upon which our definition of analyticity is based—what may be called "theoretical definition"—is not considered by Quine. Because of the differences between theoretical definitions, on the one hand, and lexical definitions, explications, and notational definitions, on the other, and because Quine's arguments against the analytic-synthetic distinction are based on features of the latter three types of definition that are not features of theoretical definition, his arguments do not carry over to an account of analyticity formulated in terms of a theoretical definition in linguistic theory.

Theoretical definitions state the structure of concepts within the framework of a system of principles that connect the definiens to sets of predictions about the phenomena that the system of principles, the theory, is designed to handle. Thus, theoretical definition avoids the inherent difficulty with explication that no way has yet been devised to decide when a departure from the meaning of the explicandum is an improvement and when it is simply a failure on the part of the explicatum to succeed in capturing a significant aspect of the meaning of the explicandum. Like lexical definitions, theoretical definitions in linguistics can be used to describe the empirical facts about a natural language in the form of confirmable hypotheses about grammatical

[79] W. V. Quine, *From a Logical Point of View,* pp. 24–27.

regularities. Yet, unlike lexical definitions, theoretical definitions do not describe such facts by defining one term by others from the same language (or another language). Theoretical definitions do not express hypotheses about a language in the form of statements that assert the synonymy of such terms and expressions. Rather—and this is the significant difference—theoretical definitions define terms *on the basis of constructs from a theory*, in the present case, the theory which expresses what is common to natural languages in the form of a definition of the notion 'natural language'. Terms from a natural language are defined by dictionary entries which represent each of their senses in the form of a theoretical construction, a reading, that is composed not of words from that language but of symbols expressing language-independent constructs, i.e., semantic markers, drawn from the theoretical vocabulary of empirical linguistics.

There are several reasons why the semantic component of a grammar must employ theoretical definition rather than lexical definition. One is that defining words by pairing them with synonymous expressions in the same language (or even a different one; it makes no difference here) cannot provide an account of their meaning. Such pairings say no more than that the meaning of this or that word is the same as the meaning of some expression without at all saying what the meaning of either is. They are thus no more illuminating about meaning than the statement that two species have the same sensory organ is about the nature of that organ. Another reason is this. Being expressions in the same natural language, the definientia of lexical definitions will have, in general, the same semantic properties and relations that other words and expressions do. In particular, given the fact that practically every word in a natural language is ambiguous, which one can easily verify by consulting any standard reference dictionary like Webster's, practically every definiens of a lexical definition will be ambiguous, too. Accordingly, lexical definitions cannot give *the* meaning of their definienda. To do this would require some way of disambiguating the definiens antecedently, some way of identifying the proper sense from among the various senses of the definiens and indicating that it alone is the sense of the definiendum; and this cannot be done by further lexical definitions for just the reason that requires such disambiguation in the first place. These and other reasons make it necessary to resist the extension of lexical definition, which has its proper place in ordinary reference dictionaries, to theoretical semantics.

Because theoretical definition defines a sense of a word in terms of a vocabulary of theoretical constructs (semantic markers), synonymy relations are affirmed on the basis of sameness of semantic representation, i.e., where the readings correlated with the two terms or expressions are formally identical. Synonymy relations are not affirmed by the institution of a definitional connection between one term or expression from a natural language and another, as is the case in lexical definition. A case of meaning inclusion, such as "male" and "bachelor," is affirmed when the semantic markers in the

reading that represents one item all appear in the reading that represents the meaning of the other. Con-
versely, such formal relations, on the basis of which we
affirm or deny that a particular linguistic construction
has one or another semantic property or relation, provide the abstract conditions that serve as definienda for
the semantic properties and relations *synonymous
with, analytic,* and so on.

Let us now look at how the differences between
theoretical definition and those types of definition considered by Quine which prevent Quine's arguments
from applying to our account of analyticity. We can
agree, at the outset, that Quine is correct in what he
says about the possibility of defining synonyms as constructions that are interchangeable *salva veritate.*
Something stronger is, of course, needed, and it is interchangeability *salva analyticitate.* We agree, further,
that philosophers who sought to explain the notion of
analyticity on the basis of the notion of synonymy, cannot define "synonymy" in terms of "analyticity." But
such circularity is not a necessary feature of any attempt to define these notions, but only a feature of
certain attempts to use lexical definition to define
them. Employing theoretical definition instead enables
us to avoid the circularity of trying to define analyticity
in terms of logical truth and synonymy, and then synonymy in terms of interchangeability *salva analyticitate.* Within this new framework, "analytic,"
"synonymous," etc., do not themselves appear in the
definienda of the definition of any of these semantic
concepts. Each such concept is defined in terms of cer-

tain formal features of the readings for sentences and their constituents, more precisely, in terms of formal conditions on semantically interpreted underlying phrase markers. For example, above we defined "analytic sentence" without any appeal to such terms as "synonymous," etc.

This method of defining semantic properties and relations is general. Every semantic property and relation will be defined on the same basis, i.e., in terms of a configuration of symbols in semantically interpreted underlying phrase markers. Thus semantic theory defines semantic properties and relations as in (5.19)-(5.27). Of course, as things presently stand, there are semantic properties and relations that have not been so defined within semantic theory, but my claim is not that semantic theory is complete. My claim is that semantic theory offers sufficiently rich conceptual apparatus for representing semantic structure to enable us, with sufficient ingenuity, to set up adequate definitions for all semantic properties and relations.

Carnap's conception of semantical rules (and meaning postulates) is criticized by Quine essentially on two counts. First, there is what I shall refer to as the *generality criticism:* that the notion which should be defined is "*S* is analytic for *L*" for variable "*S*" and "*L*," but that Carnap does not so define it. Second, there is what I shall call the *explanation criticism:* that, besides a specification of the analytic statements of a language, we require some account of just what is attributed to them by marking them as analytic. These criticisms establish the inadequacy of Carnap's treatment of analyticity.

Neither, however, carries over to my treatment of

analyticity, synonymy, etc. The generality criticism
does not carry over because, on my account, semantic
properties' and relations are defined within linguistic
theory. Accordingly, their definitions have the status of
hypotheses about what all languages have in common,
and, hence, each semantic property or relation is
defined for variable *"L."*[80] Furthermore, unlike Carnap's account, where some analytic statements qualify
as such by virtue of being listed under the heading
"analytic," on my account, the concept "analytic" is
defined in terms of a formal condition such that *any*
sentence whose semantically interpreted underlying
phrase marker satisfies it is analytic. The same is true of
other semantic properties and relations, and, hence,
semantic concepts are defined for variable *"S,"* too.

The explanation criticism does not carry over either.
Quine rightly says of Carnap's semantical rules that
"the rules contain the word 'analytic', which we do not
understand! We understand what expressions the rules
attribute analyticity to, but we do not understand what
the rules attribute to those expressions."[81] On my treatment, however, "analytic" is defined in a way that tells
us what is attributed to a sentence so marked: being a

[80]These definitions are not restricted to any particular language, since a
linguistic description, or generative grammar, of a natural language describes each of its sentences in terms of a set of semantically interpreted
underlying phrase markers, and the formal features referred to in the definitions of semantic properties and relations are features of readings and semantic markers in general (rather than specific symbols that might appear
in some but not all descriptions). Of course, in order to obtain predictions
about the semantic properties and relations of particular sentences in a
given natural language, these definitions must be applied to the semantically
interpreted underlying phrase markers for those sentences, but this is only
a matter of specifying the values of the variables S and L in a particular case.

[81]W. V. Quine, "Two Dogmas of Empiricism," p. 33.

proposition that is linguistically secured against false-hood by virtue of having its truth conditions as part of its presupposition.

So as not to attribute to Quine a position that he may not actually hold, let us distinguish between "Quine of the printed word" and "Quine of legendary fame."[82] Henceforth, unless otherwise indicated, I will be talk-ing only about the latter Quine. This Quine is reputed to deny any analytic–synthetic distinction on the basis of an argument which might be put as follows: "Insofar as one can construct semantic interpretations for sen-tences of natural languages, as envisaged, one can make a sharp analytic–synthetic distinction *in linguistic the-ory,* but the definitions for 'analytic', 'synonymous', etc., in linguistic theory are of use only if such semantic interpretations can be set up on a sound empirical basis. Otherwise they are merely empty exercises in defini-tion. But there is no such basis for them." Thus the focus of Quine's skepticism shifts from the general concepts 'analytic', 'synonymous', etc., to the semantic represen-tations of the sentences and constituents on the basis of which these general concepts are to be applied. In terms of a specific case, the point can be put as follows. If the readings for the subject and predicate of (6.16) are the way they are alleged to be, then (6.16) is ana-lytic, but what is the evidential basis for the claim that these readings are the way they are alleged to be?

---

[82]By "Quine of legendary fame" I do not mean Quine at all. I use this device as a way of talking about certain prevalent views stemming from misinterpretations of Quine, which are now part of the folklore of our sub-ject.

The general question is how we tell whether a reading correctly represents the meaning of the construction to which it is assigned. Let us start with a straightforward answer. A semantic description, as part of a generative gammar, is a theory about the semantic structure of a language. The readings given in the semantic description for sentences and other syntactically complex constituents come from the readings that the dictionary provides for their component morphemes. Thus the question is basically about how we decide on the correctness of these lexical readings. Since a lexical reading is a hypothesis about the structure of a sense of a morpheme, one part of the evidential basis for a lexical reading will be considerations to the effect that it helps us state true empirical regularities at the lexical level. The question "Should one reading for 'bachelor' contain the semantic marker (Male)?" becomes "Does the reading for 'bachelor' that contains (Male) help us state an empirical regularity?"

The inclusion of a semantic marker in lexical readings for different morphemes is the manner in which a grammar states a regularity over those morphemes. The lexical items whose readings contain this semantic marker are *ipso facto* grouped together as semantically similar in the respect indicated by the semantic marker, i.e., as in (6.29). Moreover, the inclusion of (Male) in the lexical reading for the "unmarried-adult-man" sense of "bachelor" and its exclusion from the lexical reading for the "person-having-a-degree-for-completion-of-the-first-four-years-of-college" sense enables us to state one of the empirical differences between these senses. Again, hypotheses worked into a theory as integrated parts of the theory can be tested in various indirect ways by virtue of the ways in which they are systematically interconnected with other parts of the theory. For example, since (Male) and (Female) are antonymous semantic markers,[83] we can use this reading for "bachelor" to mark

(6.39)   My mother is a bachelor

as contradictory on one of its senses. Furthermore, because (Male) helps to distinguish different senses of "bachelor," it helps to mark (6.39) as semantically ambiguous. Also, it helps us mark (6.40)

(6.40)   Someone is a bachelor

as entailed by (6.41),

(6.41)   Someone is a male.

Since this lexical reading helps us mark these and other semantic properties and relations, there is certainly empirical evidence for the claim that one reading of "bachelor" should have (Male) occur in it, and this evidence is, in turn, also evidence that (6.16) is analytic.

We might suppose that we can rest our case with the observation that the above treatment of "bachelor" can serve as a model; for the treatment of any other examples about which the same methodological question is raised. But for the Quine of legendary fame this

---

[83]Antonymous semantic markers reflect in their formal structure the logical incompatability between the concepts they represent. Cf. J. J. Katz, *The Philosophy of Language* (New York: Harper & Row, 1966), pp. 118–204.

straightforward answer will not do. "How do you know," he will ask, "that (6.39) is semantically ambiguous and contradictory on one of its senses, or that (6.41) entails (6.40), or that (6.16) is analytic?" To this, we would answer that such facts are obtained from intuitive judgments speakers make about the sentences; these judgments constitute our data.

Quine's rejoinder will concern how we obtain such data, and he will ask two questions. First, he will want to know how we deal with cases that are unclear because speakers are unable to make definite judgments about them. For example, we can expect speakers to be somewhat confused about whether or not

(6.42)   Whales are fish

is analytic, or even expect that they might make a wrong judgment about this case.[84] But here we can reply that, as indicated in the last paragraph of Chapter 4, we do not need to have clear-cut judgments about a given case to have sound evidence on which to assert its analyticity, since we can bring indirect evidence to bear on it. That is, the virtue of semantic theory is that it interrelates semantic concepts, and, thus, permits us to decide on the character of an unclear case by theoretical triangulation from clear cases of sentences having other semantic properties and relations. Let us give an example of this in connection with (6.42). We

---

[84]Goodman says in *The Structure of Appearance* (Cambridge: Harvard University Press, 1951), pp. 5–6, "To most of us 'fish' unquestionably applies to whales; if the biologist says that whales are not fish, his use of 'fish' differs from ours."

assume that "fishing" and "whaling" are, respectively, an activity in which one tries to catch fish and an activity in which one tries to catch whales, so that "fishing" and "whaling" differ semantically in just the way that "fish" and "whale" do. Now, "but"-conjunction is governed by a semantic restriction that the conjoined expressions contrast semantically. If no semantic contact occurs, the whole conjunction is semantically anomalous. For example,

(6.43)   I went fishing but caught a fish (bass, pike, etc.) instead

(6.44)   I went whaling but caught a whale (baleen, sperm, etc.) instead

are both semantically anomalous because the object of the second clause in each makes what was caught something of the same type as that which the speaker was trying to catch, or a subtype of that type. To avoid semantic anomaly, the type indicated by the object in the second clause must be a contrasting type. Thus,

(6.45)   I went fishing but caught an old shoe instead
(6.46)   I went whaling but caught an octopus instead

are both nonanomalous sentences. But

(6.47)   I went fishing but caught a whale instead
(6.48)   I went whaling but caught a fish instead

are also nonanomalous. From this we can conclude that whales are not a type of fish, from the viewpoint of English. This can be reflected in the lexical reading for "whale" only if that reading does not contain the semantic markers that represent the concept of a fish, and, hence, (6.42) will not be marked as analytic, even though there may be no clear-cut judgment to this effect about (6.42) *per se.*[85]

Second, Quine will want to know whether, in clear cases, the questions we ask speakers will have to contain technical terms of semantic theory. "Must speakers understand what such technical terms as 'semantically ambiguous', 'contradictory', 'entails', and 'analytic' mean before they can answer reliably?" The answer to this question is a categorical "no." It is possible to obtain the relevant data without invoking such technical terms in framing the questions that are put to speakers and thereby presupposing that speakers know what they mean. One test that avoids such circularity is this. We present speakers with short lists of sentences. List A contains only sentences that are clear cases of what we would regard as analytic. Lists B, C, D, etc., contain clear cases of sentences that are not analytic, but, say, respectively, synthetic, contradictory, anomalous, etc. Then, we give the speakers a batch of sentences of all

---

[85]Another case of the same kind is the following:
  (i) John caught a sperm and Bill caught a whale also
  (ii) John caught a bass and Bill caught a whale also
  (iii) John caught a whale and Bill caught a whale also
  (iv) John caught a whale and Bill caught a fish also
"Also" in such constructions has the semantic requirement that the object of the second sentence structure has a reading identical to the reading of the object in the first, or one that is included in the reading of the object in the first. Hence, (ii) and (iv) are both semantically deviant, and this fact is further evidence for the claim that (6.42) is not analytic.

sorts and ask them to place these sentences on the lists to which they belong. Each sentence is to be put on the list with whose members it is most similar. If this experiment is conducted properly and if the predictions of the semantic component of the grammar makes match the actual sorting performed by the speakers (cases that are put on list A are those and only those that are predicted to be analytic, and so on), then we can claim that we have evidence, obtained in a quite unobjectionable fashion, in favor of the semantic component.

However, the qualification that the experiment be conducted properly is extremely important. If the controls used in the experiment ensure that the members of the short lists A, B, C, etc., are sufficiently different from one another in the appropriate respects, then there will be no spurious common features that might lead speakers to classify sentences on the basis of irrelevant linguistic properties (e.g., in the case of list A, on the basis of some other linguistic property than analyticity). Positive results in this experiment can be interpreted to mean that the judgments of the speakers reflect a recognition of the analyticity of the sentences concerned. We can say, then, that our definition of analyticity, which enabled us to predict the outcome of the experiment, describes the concept of analyticity employed by the speakers as their implicit criterion for identifying analytic sentences, i.e., for differentiating those of the test sentences that are similar to the members of list A from those that are not similar to them. We can say this on the grounds that, if we make the assumption that this is their criterion, we obtain the best explanation of the behavioral data obtained in the experiment. Since it is just this sort of basis on which theories in other sciences are justified, it ought to satisfy even the Quine of legendary fame.[86]

[86]Quine has replied to these arguments in his article, "On a Suggestion of Katz," *The Journal of Philosophy*, vol. XLIV, No. 2, (February 2, 1967), 52–54, and I have replied to his replies in "Unpalatable Recipes for Buttering Parsnips," and in *Semantic Theory*, ch. 6.

7.

Conceptions of
the Philosophy of Language

---◅◦∞◦▻---

Philosophy of language in the first half of this century
has been dominated by two schools of thought. One,
arising out of the work of the early Wittgenstein and
the Vienna Circle, is logical positivism, and the other,
arising out of the work of the later Wittgenstein, Moore,
and Ryle, is ordinary language philosophy. Both schools
proposed *linguistic* approaches to the understanding
of logical form and philosophical problems in general.
Both advocated that attempts to answer traditional philosophical questions be based on knowledge of the linguistic form which these questions and their answers
should assume. Both took this position because they
thought that an uncritical and uninformed reliance on
language was responsible for the impasse that philosophy had gotten itself into in metaphysics. Gustav Bergmann, a logical empiricist, once gave the following
account of common ground that logical empiricists and
ordinary language philosophers share:

All linguistic philosophers talk about the world by means of talking about a suitable language. This is the linguistic turn [that philosophy has taken in the first half of this century], the fundamental gambit as to method, on which ordinary and ideal language philosophers agree. Equally fundamentally, they disagree on what is in this sense a 'language' and what makes it 'suitable'. Clearly one may execute the turn. The question is why one should. Why is it not merely a tedious roundabout? I shall mention three reasons. . . . First. Words are used either ordinarily (commonsensically) or philosophically [technically]. On this distinction, above all, the method rests. The prelinguistic philosophers did not make it. Yet they used words philosophically. *Prima facie* such uses are unintelligible. They require commonsensical explication. The method insists that we provide it. . . . Second. Much of the paradox, absurdity, and opacity of prelinguistic philosophy stems from failure to distinguish between speaking and speaking about speaking. Such failure, or confusion, is harder to avoid than one may think. The method is the safest way of avoiding it. Third. Some things any conceivable language merely shows. Not that these things are literally "ineffable"; rather, the proper (and safe) way of speaking about them is to speak about (the syntax and interpretation of a) language.[87]

These schools differed in their conception of how to guarantee that the language they talk about will be "suitable," i.e., of the kind of linguistic knowledge that provides the proper formulation of a philosophical question and the most fruitful prospects for gaining its

[87]G. Bergmann, *Logic and Reality* (Madison: University of Wisconsin Press, 1964), p. 177.

answer. Logical positivists believed that the formulation of philosophical questions in the idiom of natural language led to hopeless confusions and thus that philosophers should undertake to construct an ideal, artificial language into which sentences of a natural language could be translated if they are either nonphilosophical sentences about matters of fact or mathematical truth or philosophical sentences whose translation reveals their linguistic character. Every other philosophical sentence would be untranslatable, thereby marking it as expressing a meaningless piece of speculative metaphysics. Some logical positivists saw the construction of such ideal, artificial languages as a way of reforming natural languages, and others saw it as a way of dispensing with natural languages in philosophy. Both sought to construct such language to exhibit their claim that philosophical sentences are about language or nothing, and both hoped that, on the positive side, an ideal language would do for philosophy what the symbolic language of mathematics and logic had done for science.

Ordinary language philosophers also believed that the formulation of philosophical questions in the idiom of natural language led to confusion. They, however, believed that it was both unnecessary and impossible to circumvent natural language by resorting to the construction of artificial languages. As P.F. Strawson once remarked:

> [The aim of clarifying philosophical problems that motivates the construction of an ideal language] will seem

empty, unless the results achieved have some bearing on the typical philosophical problems and difficulties which arise concerning the concepts to be clarified. Now these problems . . . have their roots in ordinary, unconstructed concepts, in the elusive, deceptive modes of functioning of unformalized linguistic expressions. . . . If the clear mode of functioning of the constructed concepts is to cast light on problems and difficulties rooted in the unclear mode of functioning of the unconstructed concepts, then precisely the ways in which the constructed concepts are connected with and depart from the unconstructed concepts must be plainly shown. And how can *this* result be achieved without accurately describing the modes of functioning of the unconstructed concepts? But this task is precisely the task of describing the logical behavior of the linguistic expressions of natural languages; and may *by itself* achieve the sought-for resolution of the problems and difficulties rooted in the elusive, deceptive mode of functioning of unconstructed concepts.[88]

Thus ordinary language philosophers saw the task of linguistic philosophy to lie in the clarification of the ordinary concepts that give rise to philosophical puzzles. The method they adopted of achieving such clarification was essentially the Wittgensteinian method of examining the ways that speakers use their language.

We have already considered Wittgenstein's reasons for abandoning the idea that concepts are to be understood as the meanings that give "cognitive life" to oth-

---

[88]P. F. Strawson, "Carnap's Views on Constructed Systems vs. Natural Languages in Analytic Philosophy," in *The Philosophy of Rudolph Carnap*, P. A. Schilpp, ed. (La Salle: Open Court, 1963), pp. 512–513.

erwise dead pieces of orthography and accepting in its place the idea that concepts are to be understood in terms of the uses to which words are put in actual employment of languages in everyday life. We must now indicate how this doctrine provided a method for ordinary language philosophy and a conception of philosophical inquiry.

The primary feature of this method and its associated conception of philosophical inquiry is that philosophy is in no way like theoretical science. If there is no underlying conceptual reality to language, then philosophical inquiry does not proceed in the manner of a theoretical science. It does not and attempt to account for the heterogeneity of phenomena in terms of a theory that represents it as the surface confluence of distinct features of a highly systematic underlying reality. Explanation, as the reduction of heterogeneity at the surface to order beneath, can play no role in philosophical inquiry. Thus Wittgenstein writes:

> . . . we may not advance any kind of theory. There must not be anything hypothetical in our considerations. We must do away with all *explanations,* and description alone must take its place. And this description gets its power of illumination—i.e. its purpose—from the philosophical problems. These are, of course, not empirical problems; they are solved, rather, by looking into the workings of our language, and that in such a way as to make us recognize those workings: *in spite of* an urge to misunderstand them. The problems are solved, not by giving new information, but by arranging what we have always known. Philosophy is a battle against the

bewitchment of our intelligence by means of language.[89]

The "battle" is waged by attempting to show how a philosophical problem arises through the departure from the ordinary use of words. Thus:

> When philosophers use a word—'knowledge', 'being', 'object', 'I', 'proposition', 'name'—and try to grasp the *essence* of the thing, one must always ask oneself: is the word ever actually used in this way in the language-game which is its original home?—
>
> What we do is to bring words back from their metaphysical to their everyday usage.[90]

As radically different as logical positivism and ordinary language philosophy are, they share a critical presupposition. This is the assumption, upon which taxonomic linguistics was also predicated, that natural languages have no underlying reality, that their surface structure and the public aspects of the way their words and sentences are used are all there is to take account of in studying them.

As a consequence of making this assumption, logical positivists thought that natural languages were unsystematic, irregular, and logically imperfect. Carnap, one of the leaders of this school, once wrote:

> In consequence of the unsystematic and logically imperfect structure of the natural word-languages (such as

---

[89]L. Wittgenstein, *Philosophical Investigations*, p. 47$^\text{e}$
[90]*Ibid.*, p. 48$^\text{e}$.

German or Latin), the statement of their formal rules of formation and [logical] transformation would be so complicated that it would hardly be feasible in practice.[91]

And further:

The fact that natural languages allow the formation of meaningless sequences of words without violating the rules of grammar, indicates that grammatical syntax is, from a logical point of view, inadequate. If grammatical syntax corresponded exactly to logical syntax, pseudo-statements could not arise. If grammatical syntax differentiated not only the word-categories of nouns, adjectives, verbs, conjunctions, etc., but within each of these categories made the further distinctions that are logically indispensable, then no pseudo-statements could be formed. . . . In a correctly constructed language . . . considerations of grammar would already eliminate [nonsensical sequences of words] as it were automatically. . . . It follows that if our thesis that the statements of metaphysics are pseudo-statements is justifiable, then metaphysics could not even be expressed in a logically constructed language. This is the great philosophical importance of the task, which at present occupies the logicians, of building a logical syntax.[92]

It is clear that the second claim is based on—and stands or falls by—the notion that grammatical analysis of a sentence simply classifies its constituent words and phrases into the traditional syntactic categories of

[91]R. Carnap, *The Logical Syntax of Language* (London: Routledge & Kegan Paul, 1937), p. 2.

[92]R. Carnap, "The Elmination of Metaphysics," in *Logical Positivism*, A. J. Ayer, ed. (Glencoe, Ill.: The Free Press, 1959), p. 68.

noun, verb, adjective, conjunction, and so on. But since this is precisely the notion of grammatical analysis (and of its scope and limits) adopted by taxonomic grammarians, this second claim should be recast to read: No *taxonomic analysis* of the structure of sentences in natural languages ˙can reveal the logical forms necessary for stating the rules of inference which codify valid argumentation.

With *this* claim we are in wholehearted agreement. In fact, the extended argument in the first part of this monograph to establish that there is an underlying level of grammatical structure which cannot be accounted for by a taxonomic grammar establishes just this version of the second claim. However, this version, though true and supported by a wealth of examples where surface grammatical form does not coincide with deep logical form, does not support the case for artificial languages as necessary replacements for natural languages. The philosopher who thinks such a replacement necessary for purposes of rational thought also makes the further, and false, assumption that taxonomic grammars are the only type available. If they were, it would be reasonable to argue that the best grammar can do is not good enough, and that therefore an artificial language of one sort or another is needed to exhibit the aspects of logical form that are unmarked in grammatical analysis. But since a conception of the grammar of the sentences that can account for aspects of logical form that are unmarked in a taxonomic analysis of surface structure has been available since the time of the Port-Royal grammarians, the argument for the need of artificial languages collapses completely. Were natural languages amorphous products of rationally uncontrolled cultural evolution, as an empiricist would automatically think, one could expect the metaphysical worst of them. The scruples of ordinary language philosophers to one side, one would be justified in seeking to construct an artificial language, built on the model of a logico-mathematical system, that would be a more suitable vehicle for philosophical reasoning. But since the amorphousness is only an artifact of the way that linguistic structure has been traditionally represented, the case logical positivists put forth to support their claims on behalf of ideal artificial languages has little to recommend it.

Ordinary language philosophers were led by this common presupposition to eschew the attempt to theorize about the structure of natural language and to concentrate their efforts on the attempt to describe the details of linguistic use. The result, after a few decades of such analyses, was an enormous number of highly particular facts about how words and sentences of English are normally used, but no principles that give insight into the nature of linguistic structure.

Therefore, it is natural to hope that transformational grammar in showing the inadequacy of this common assumption would pave the way for a more promising philosophy of language. The hope that transformational grammar holds out to philosophers is that by revealing the structure underlying surface irregularity, it will provide information about the logical form of sentences that is useful in formulating answers to traditional philosophical questions.

Let us try to frame a conception of philosophy of language based upon the transformational theory of language. The special task of philosophy of language, which distinguishes it from other branches of philosophy, is that it seeks to shed light on the structure of conceptual knowledge on the basis of insights into the structure of the languages in which such knowledge is expressed and communicated. A conception of the philosophy of language, therefore, begins with some notion of (i) what natural languages are and how best to study them, (ii) what relation obtains between linguistic structure and the concepts that give rise to philosophical problems, and (iii) how the results of the study of natural languages can be relevant to the formulation of solutions to philosophical problems. As we have observed, a conception of the philosophy of language based on transformational theory takes an entirely different view of what language and the study of language is from that taken by logical positivism and ordinary language philosophy, the principle difference being that it sees their references to linguistic structure as references to the surface appearance of languages and its own references as references to an underlying reality where the significant linguistic relationships are found. Thus it differs sharply with both earlier schools of thought at the most fundamental level.

There are, however, areas of agreement with each of these schools. Our approach sides with logical positivism in seeking a theory of linguistic structure that takes the form of a formalized system, though it requires that the formalized theory be a theory of linguistic structure in natural languages, not an artifical language that can have whatever properties its maker desires it to have. Thus the formal rules of linguistic theory must represent the real relations in language that underly their connection of sound and meaning, and they must be open to empirical verification in terms of facts that come to light in the linguist's field work. Accordingly, our approach sides with ordinary language philosophy in that it insists on "accurately describing the modes of functioning of the unconstructed concepts" in terms of "precisely . . . describing the logical behavior of the linguistic expression of natural languages." The empirical pheneomena of natural language are both the starting point in the erection of a linguistic theory and the terminal point in its verification. But description by itself is not enough. Description is the first stage in constructing explanations that posit linguistic structures which cannot be observed in speech. Description provides the evidence for such underlying linguistic structures which in turn is explained by a grammatical theory of underlying linguistic structures.

Accordingly, we can say that our conception of the philosophy of language has the virtues of both logical positivism and ordinary language philosophy without incurring the vices of either. In this conception, the virtues of formalization and theory are combined with those of a realistic concern with actual languages and careful description of linguistic structure. Thus the conception is free of the vices of disregarding the character of natural languages to erect artificial languages as prescriptions for usage, on the one hand, and on the other, of restricting linguistic analysis to informal descriptions of usage that do not uncover explanatory principles of linguistic form.

The conception of the philosophy of language does not have to claim that there is always a relation between linguistic structure and concepts which gives rise to philosophical problems. It can give qualified endorsement to the doctrine that philosophical problems are linguistic in nature: It can claim that linguistic considerations enter into every philosophical problem but reserve judgment as to how significant the linguistic considerations are in the final analysis. It can take the position that by pursuing a study of natural language within the framework of transformational grammar and by drawing the proper inferences about the structure of conceptual knowledge from the results of such a study, the linguistic doctrine about philosophical problems is itself tested. The scope of such inferences can itself determine which philosophical problems admit of a linguistic solution and the extent to which linguistic considerations enter into the solution of other problems.

To fully specify our conception of the philosophy of language we need to give a more precise account of the relation between linguistic structure and the philosophical matters on which it bears. As we see it, this relation is one that holds primarily between the universals of language and the concerns about which philosophical questions arise. Therefore on this conception,

the most significant aspect of linguistics for philosophical investigation is the theory of grammar (the theory
of language). This view rests on two assumptions. First,
the philosophical problems that can be dealt with linguistically are ones that depend on features of the underlying reality of language. Second, the features of the
underlying reality of language on which they depend
are universal. If both assumptions are generally right,
then the philosophy of language must look to the theory
of linguistic universals for the concepts and principles
to use in constructing solutions to philosophical problems.[93]

[93]This conception of the philosophy of language was first presented at a
symposium on 'Philosophy and Linguistics' at the 1965 meetings of the
American Philosophical Association, and published under the title "The
Relevance of Linguistics to Philosophy," *The Journal of Philosophy*, Vol.
LXII, No. 20, (October 20, 1965), 590–602. In this paper I express the
relevance in this way:

> A number of philosophical problems can be represented as questions
> about the nature of language, and . . . so presented, they can be solved
> by conceptual constructions found in linguistic theory. [My thesis is] that
> conceptual constructions, initially devised to enable linguistic theory to
> state uniformities systematically, also fulfill the conditions on solutions to
> philosophical problems. [If this is so] . . . then linguistics is not incidentally
> pertinent to philosophy in the way that philosophy bears upon the clarifi-
> cation of methodology and theory construction in linguistics, but is di-
> rectly relevant in the same way that philosophical theories themselves
> are.

Zeno Vendler, one of the commentators at that symposium, presented an
alternative conception of the relevance of linguistics to philosophy. He
wrote (same issue, p. 590):

> What [Katz] consistently overlooks is the possibility that the linguistic
> data themselves, obtainable by means of an advanced theory of language,
> might have philosophical significance. Conceptual investigations based
> upon facts of language cannot but profit by a more systematic presenta-
> tion and deeper understanding of these facts. What Oxford philosophers

did in an informal manner, what Austin tried to develop into a 'linguistic phenomenology', can be pursued and made more cogent and powerful by drawing upon the resources of contemporary linguistics. Just one illustration. Had Austin known transformational grammar, he would not have been misled into assimilating facts to events by the possibility of saying, for instance, both that the collapse of the Germans is an event and that the collapse of the Germans is a fact. For he would have realized that the phrase "the collapse of the Germans" is transformationally ambiguous. . . .

Now I would not deny that linguistic data can be of some philosophical significance, but to bring out the contrast between Vendler's conception of the relevance of linguistics and mine, I would argue that the philosophical significance of linguistic data as Vendler conceives it is of an extremely low order, and, even so, their use depends on a theory of language. Consider Vendler's example of the ambiguous phrase
 (i) The collapse of the Germans
     which has an event-sense, as in
 (ii) The collapse of the Germans was slow and ended in 1945
     and a fact-sense, as in
 (iii) The collapse of the Germans was not accepted by Hitler
The only philosophical relevance for the Austin-Strawson debate on truth of the linguistic data that points up this ambiguity in (i) is that such data would show Austin to have committed a simple fallacy of ambiguity in one of his arguments. Consequently, their relevance is of a very minor sort and hardly of the same order as that of concepts or principles of the theory of grammar that provide a solution to a philosophical problem. The relevance Vendler claims for linguistic data is, therefore, like the relevance of the old-fashioned discussions of rhetoric found in the early chapters of elementary logic texts.

Vendler might still argue that, despite their low order of relevance, appropriate linguistic data nevertheless provide a philosopher with stronger support for a distinction than is provided by his own intuitive grasp of the language. This, I take it, is what he means when he says (again, same issue, p. 604):

Certainly one *could* arrive at the same distinction by simply collecting data in an intuitive fashion. The point is, though, that, given a satisfactory theory of nominalizations, these data can be collected by simply following a routine, and, once found, they fall into a consistent pattern indicating an unequivocal conclusion.

But bringing the complex apparatus of nominalization transformations to bear in order to show that Austin failed to notice that (i) is ambiguous and that his argument thus equivocates is like using a hydrogen bomb to eliminate a patch of poison ivy.

Be this as it may, however, if linguistic data are to "fall into a consistent pattern indicating an unequivocal conclusion," they must become evidence for a set of nominalization transformations that predict the ambiguity of (i). That is, there must be a set of nominalization transformations that predict these data (thereby providing adequate empirical reason to accept these transformations as sound grammatical rules) and that assign two appropriately different underlying phrase makers to (i) (thereby showing that (i) is syntactically ambiguous). Otherwise, the use of linguistic data will not enable the philosopher to do anything he could not do without the aid of linguistics, for unaided by linguistics, he could say that events but not facts can be sudden or gradual, while facts but not events can be believed or disbelieved. He could thus conclude that since (i) can refer to something sudden or gradual or something believed or disbelieved, it must be ambiguous between a fact-sense and an event-sense. If Vendler's approach is to succeed in enabling the linguistically sophisticated philosopher to go beyond the linguistically unsophisticated philosopher in the way suggested, the use of linguistic data must presuppose a set of transformational rules, and so a theory of grammar that characterizes such rules and explain the way an assignment of two (or more) underlying phrase markers to a sentence represents it as syntactically ambiguous.

Another alternative conception of the relevance of linguistics to philosophy is one that regards the grammar of a particular natural language rather than the linguistic data as of primary relevance. The difference between this conception and mine is that this one restricts the concepts and principles that philosophy may borrow from linguistics for the formulation of a solution to a philosophical problem to those in the particular grammar. Thus it represents a relativization of the solution to the language in question. My conception, on the other hand, bases the solution to a philosophical problem on concepts and principles that express universals of language and thus it avoids such a stultifying relativization. While Plato and Aristotle wrote in Greek, Descartes in Latin and French, Kant in German, and Locke, Berkeley, and Hume in English, the philosophical problems they wrote about were language independent questions about a common body of conceptual knowledge. Thus it is just as absurd to say that the solution to the problem of causality, memory, *a priori* knowledge, innate ideas, or other minds is such-and-such *in English* (or French or any other particular language) as to say that a broken back is such-and-such a condition among Chinese (or any other particular nationality). Accordingly, anyone who accepts this alternative conception and the relativization that it entails faces a dilemma. Either he cautiously puts forth a solution obtained by examining one or another particular natural language as a language *de*pendent solution, in which case he will be addressing himself to the wrong problem since philosophical problems require language *in*dependent solutions, or he rashly puts forth the solution as a language *in*dependent one, in which case he cannot offer what will be required for its empirical substantiation since, *ex hypothesi*, he restricts his evidence to the data from only one language.

There is a rather ironic turn of events in store for philosophy in this and the next few decades if the conception of the philosophy of language presented in this monograph correctly represents the recent "linguistic turn" in philosophy. We may see the philosophies of language of Logical Empiricism and Ordinary Language Philosophy replaced by a philosophy of language based on a scientific theory of universal linguistic structure, concerned with uncovering properties of knowledge and mind on the basis of philosophically relevant aspects of the underlying reality of natural languages. If this happens, the linguistic turn taken by philosophy in the first half of the twentieth century will have turned back on itself, reintroducing the very metaphysical issues whose banishment from philosophy was initially proclaimed as the rationale for the turn to linguistic philosophy.